JUDAISM — FOSSIL OR FERMENT?

JUDAISM
Fossil or Ferment?

by

ELIEZER BERKOVITS

PHILOSOPHICAL LIBRARY
New York

PRINTED IN THE UNITED STATES OF AMERICA

TABLE OF CONTENTS

PREFACE

THIS WORK has grown out of an attempt to ascertain the opinions of the English historian Arnold J. Toynbee on Judaism and the Jewish people as they may be found in his monumental *A Study of History*.

Toynbee's attitude to Judaism and Jewry is determined by his general interpretation of history. It is for this reason that Jews have to come to grips with it. Toynbee dismisses Judaism and Jewry, with an awe-inspiring claim to scholarship, on the grounds that they have failed in their endeavor to solve the problems of human existence. This is a challenge aimed at the very heart of all Israel. If Toynbee is right, there is no moral and spiritual justification for being a Jew. At the same time, the dilemma is Toynbee's too. For, if he is wrong on the subject of Judaism, he is wrong altogether. His interpretation of Jewish history is not at all incidental to his main theme. Judaism and Jewry represent the antithesis to the Toynbean thesis.

The Jewish student of Toynbee's great work must therefore look to his own bearings and review—and, if need be, revise—his own position. With the present volume the author has tried to meet that challenge for himself. He submits it to a wider public in the hope that it may be of help to others at a time when the meager knowledge and understanding of Judaism permit the Toynbean misrepresentations and distortions to cause confusion even among the Jewish readers of the English historian.

The present volume falls into two parts. The first deals with Toynbee's interpretation of Judaism and Jewish history up to the fall of Jerusalem in the year 69-70 c.e. With that event, according to Toynbee, the history of the Jewish people as well as that of Judaism came to an end. The second part is centered around Chapter IV, which presents Toynbee's explanation of Jewish survival after Jewry's "extinction" in the year 70 c.e. In each case the author has tried to show how Toynbee's opinions proceed from his general philosophy of history and religion. First, these specific views on Judaism and Jewish survival are analyzed on the basis of the Toynbean premises themselves and tested for their consistency and logicality. Next, the author offers a Jewish interpretation of those aspects of Judaism and Jewish history which have come under the purview of Toynbee's inquiry. Finally, the author has endeavored to show the Jewish position on the broad universal issues of man's existence and his relationship to God, over which—in the opinion of Toynbee—Judaism and the Jewish people came to grief. In the epilogue, an attempt is made to present the net result of *A Study of History* with a view to the crisis of our own times, as well as to evaluate it from a Jewish standpoint.

A Study of History is usually referred to in this book as the *Study*. The places in the *Study* from which quotations are taken are indicated in the notes by volume and page number only. Thus "V/237" refers to *A Study of History,* Volume V, page 237.

E. B.

Kislev, 5716—November, 1955.

INTRODUCTION

TOYNBEE'S CRITICISM of Judaism and Jewry is spread practically across the entire face of the ten volumes of his *Study*. This is the external mark of the intrinsic connection that exists between that author's interpretation of world history and his understanding of Judaism. Believing that he has discerned the central theme of all history, he briskly treads his path through the maze of events and occurrences. But it is his central theme which is responsible for Toynbee's preoccupation with Judaism, as well as for the facts that most of the basic principles of the *Study* are developed in innumerable—rather one-sided—debates against Judaism and the alleged aspirations of the Jewish people. The theme of universal history, according to Toynbee, is Man's Salvation. But no one who is bold enough to believe in that will ever be able to get away from Israel. He must either bless or curse—and Toynbee does both—but he cannot leave alone. The salvation of man is not only a central theological concept of Judaism, but the goal toward which, in Judaic teaching, all history is moving. It was the prophets of Israel, and they alone, who interpreted history as man's Messianic development toward his salvation. Toynbee takes over the Jewish concept but puts it to work side by side with his rejection of Judaism and of the Jewish people. No wonder that the final outcome of *A Study of History* is intellectually as well as morally insipid.[1]

Probably the most significant aspect of *A Study of History* is that it is not at all a historical work, i.e., one belonging to the discipline of the science of history. It is a philosophical and theological inquiry concerning a great deal of historical raw material. The historian Toynbee supplies the information; the philosopher and theologian Toynbee provides the interpretation. However, since Toynbee is much more historian than theologian or philosopher, he really believes that his interpretation

1. See below the Epilogue, section 2.

is derived from the facts of history; and so he lustily engages in the discovery of a considerable number of "laws" of history. But since the days of Hume and Kant no philosopher should make the mistake of thinking that "laws" can be derived from facts. That man cannot save himself and depends for his salvation on an Act of Grace by God, who in a form incarnate gives Himself to the world in order to redeem it, is Christian doctrine; and as such it will be treated with respect as the faith of their fellow men by non-Christians too. But when Toynbee adduces countless instances of human failure in history in order to distill from them the *proof* that man, on account of his intrinsic nature, will never save himself—which, by the way, is Toynbee's central thesis—then he is talking nonsense. The examples may establish the fact that, up to date, man has not succeeded in saving himself. Whether he has failed because he has blundered—and what he needs is more time to try—or because he is incapable of saving himself: on this point history remains silent. It is for the religions and philosophies of mankind to take over where history leaves off and to interpret the facts as best they may. The principles of interpretation do not emanate from history, but from philosophy, ethics, and religion. It is so in the case of Toynbee, and as it has been so in the case of all the interpreters of history, even though he does not seem to be aware of the fact. Toynbee's "laws" of history are all imported from without and applied to the facts, but not proved by them. From the point of view of historical objectivity all that one might say in their favor is that, according to Toynbee, they are not contradicted by the facts.

Toynbee's discussion of H. A. L. Fisher's approach to history is beside the point.[1] Fisher is of course right that, for the historian, history is without meaning. But this is not the same as saying that "history is bunkum." The meaning is in the interpretation, and the interpretation is never provided by history itself. Toynbee is fooling himself when he suggests that his "laws" are those of history. They are philosophical and theological concepts with whose help he attempts to bring order to the chaos of historical events. There may be dozens of others, as there indeed are, that may be equally useful as "categories"

1. See V/414.

or as "principles of selection" for the purpose of imposing some order on the "Tohu va'Bohu" of mere facts. If the "principles of selection" are to be treated as more than a mere device for the writer of history to marshal his facts coherently, if they are to be granted the solemn dignity of "laws," expressing—as in the case of Toynbee—eternal metaphysical truth, then they have validity only in so far as they may stand their ground in the realm of philosophy, ethics, or theology. But nowhere in the *Study* is the soundness of the many philosophical, meta-physical, or theological premises of Toynbee even investigated, much less established. The author of the *Study* has read widely and makes clever eclectical and literary use of his reading; it is, however, extremely doubtful that he deserves much con-sideration either as a philosopher or as a theologian.

It would be pointless to argue that the Toynbean "laws" of history might have "statistical" significance, as—indeed—Toynbee occasionally suggests. There is no need to discuss here the question whether the concept of statistical laws of modern scientific research is at all applicable—and if so to what extent —to the study of history. Whatever the verdict of the logician, scientist, or philosopher, it is certain that statistics could never yield the Toynbean pattern of world history. By their very essence statistical laws have only quantitative meaning and are, indeed, always about quantitative relationships in nature; the Toynbean "laws" are about values and metaphysical truths. Statistical laws can be put to the test of experiment: if they "work," if they are successful, they may be assumed to be valid. The validity of value concepts, on the other hand, cannot be questioned by failure in practice, nor can metaphysical truths be ascertained by facts of history.

Toynbee, for instance, spends a great amount of effort to prove how right Jesus was when he said that all who take the sword perish by the sword. Now, for a believer in Jesus, the real significance of the pronouncement lies not in the fact that it was made on the basis of experimental observation, but in the fact that its source is divine inspiration and knowledge. It is the revelation of the metaphysical truth that this world has been so established by God that those who take the sword must perish by it. Only on this account is it wrong, in all circumstances, to take the sword; he who does so acts against the Will of God. This may be true and it does make a lot of sense for the believer, but it cannot be "proved" by a study of history. It is sufficient that history should not contradict it. What Toynbee has shown—if he has done so much—is that, as far as our observations reach, all those who ever took the sword perished by the sword. Consequently, one is entitled to conclude that, for anyone who does not wish to perish, it would be foolish to take the sword, for the probability that he will perish by the sword is extremely high. But suppose that a person should enjoy being foolish and cared nothing whether he lived or perished. . . . Notwithstanding his ten volumes, Toynbee has not made the slightest contribution toward establishing more firmly among men the truth that it is ethically wrong to take the sword. All his examples show only that taking the sword is likely to lead to failure. This, however, means nothing for the question of values. If it is right to take the sword, it will be right to do so even though one is likely to perish in the action; if it is wrong to take the sword, it will remain an evil thing to do even though it may bring honor, glory, long life, and all the riches of the world. Facts know nothing of "ought" and "ought not." Ethical values and religious truth are not confirmed by success nor invalidated by failure.

The prophets of Israel did not gain their interpretation of history as historians. The meaning which they attributed to history as the gradual Messianic evolution of mankind toward salvation has its origin in their faith in God and in the logical application of that faith to the understanding of all life. Man's failure in history is, to use a phrase of Jacob Burckhardt,[1] a scandal. The scandal caused Toynbee to panic intellectually;[2] because of it he became a religious historian. The believer, however, believes not because of the scandal, but in spite of it; nor does he seek his justification in history, but in his own conscience before God.

1. See Jacob Burckhardt, *Force and Freedom,* ed. Meridian Books, N. Y. 1955, p. 234.

2. See below chapter V, section 1 and the Epilogue, section 1.

JUDAISM — FOSSIL OR FERMENT?

I. TOYNBEE'S VERSIONS OF JUDAISM AND JEWISH HISTORY

1. JUDAISM AS A HIGHER RELIGION AND THE LAPSE INTO MILITANCY

1.

IN THE OPINION of Toynbee the outstanding event in the history of the West was the rise of Christianity.[1] As in the case of all other Higher Religions, Christianity too emerged from the clash between two civilizations. Since, however, the two civilizations in question were the "Syriac" (standing here for Jewish) and the Hellenic and, especially, since Christianity was originally the answer of Jewish souls to the challenge inherent in the conflict, an understanding of Judaism and Jewish history becomes one of the keys to the understanding of the pattern and the "laws" that Mr. Toynbee believes he is able to discern in all history. The Christian response to the challenge was successful; the Jewish response, a warning failure for all generations. No wonder, therefore, that for exceedingly long stretches through nine of the ten volumes[2] of *A Study of History* the author seems to be waging a running battle against Judaism and Jewry.

It seems, though, that Judaism was not always a failure. Its fall dates from the epiphany of Christianity. Originally, Judaism represented one of the noblest manifestations of the Spirit. The Syriac civilization, the larger unit to which Israel and Judah belong according to Mr. Toynbee's method of classification, is perhaps "the most brilliant and most original representative of the species"; and of "the three great feats to its credit ... the greatest creative achievement ... was neither its discovery of the Atlantic nor its discovery of the Alphabet," the achievement of the other Syriac peoples, but its Jewish discovery

1

of God. The "particular conception of God" of the early Hebrew tribes "is common to Judaism, Zoroastrianism, Christianity, and Islam, but alien from the Egyptiac, Sumeric, Indic, and Hellenic veins of religious thought."[3] The essence of Judaism at this early stage is summed up in the Biblical tale about the Choice of Solomon. "Ask what I shall give thee," God said to the King in a dream; and Solomon asked not for riches or honor but for "an understanding heart."[4] Mr. Toynbee comments: "This fable of Solomon's Choice is a parable of the history of the Chosen People. In the power of their spiritual understanding, the Israelites surpassed the military powers of the Philistines and the maritime powers of the Phoenicians. They had not sought after those things which the Gentiles seek, but had sought first the kingdom of God; and therefore all those things were added to them. . . ."[5]

However, soon after the death of Solomon the Hebrew tribes, "betrayed by what is false within," in fratricidal warfare brought about the beginning of the breakdown of the Syriac civilization. Thus, true to the general pattern of history, this civilization too was launched toward its inevitable "Time of Troubles," which began when the Assyrian colossus, practically invited by the breakdown, marched into the Syriac arena.[6] Fortunately, this crisis turned out to be a blessing in disguise, for it was the challenge that stimulated the "Syriac" people of the Jews to respond with the most magnificent flowering of their spiritual creativity. It was in this Time of Troubles that Judaism truly developed into one of the great Higher Religions of mankind. One might single out some of the phases in this development which are discussed by Mr. Toynbee. If the breakdown is due to "what is false within," then of course it is logical to seek for salvation by what is true within or, as it may also be put, by the transference of action from the material to the spiritual level, "from the Macrocosm to the Microcosm." That, indeed, is the secret of creativity and the "sign of growth." It was the message conveyed to Socrates by his "daimonion . . . after he had grown in wisdom and had put away childish things"; it was the intuition of Lao-tse; and it was perceived in "the still small voice in which Elijah heard at last the Godhead whom he had not seen in the fire and not encountered in the earthquake and not felt in the great and strong wind which had rent the mountains and broken in pieces the rocks."[7] Later in Jewish history this experience of Elijah is crystallized by the pre-exilic prophets of Israel into the corporate response of the Jewish people to Assyrian and Babylonian militarism. It confounds the crushing military superiority of the adversary because it is not a retort "in kind," but the answer "to a physical challenge on a spiritual plane."[8] In terms of the *Study* one may discern several features in this response. It contains an explanation of the disaster that overtook the people, the reason for which—and this is decisive—is not sought in obvious external causes, like the military might of the enemy, but in guilt within, in a realization of sin and personal failure. The explanation implies acceptance of the suffering that follows from the crisis and that is translated into "understanding of the heart." It is now that Judaism develops from its stage of an "embryonic higher religion" into its maturity. In the tribulations of this Time of Troubles, Judaism "found its soul by exchanging a parochial for an ecumenical outlook." Jewry, enlightened by suffering, resigns itself "consciously to be the instrument of God's will," and is ready now to go out and meet the world with the ethos of gentleness, to captivate souls rather than to subdue empires.[9] Mr. Toynbee, developing this theme, is unstinting in his appreciation. So he says, for example:

> . . . the classical case is the spiritual experience of the Prophets of Israel and Judah in the Syriac "Time of Troubles," when these prophets discovering their truths and delivering their message, the society out of whose bosom they had arisen, and to whose members they were addressing themselves, was lying in helpless agony in the grip of the Assyrian tiger. . . . For souls whose body social was in this fearful plight, it was an heroic spiritual feat to reject the obvious and specious explanation of their misery as the work of an irresistible external force of a material kind, and to divine that, in spite of all outward appearances, it was their own sin that was the true cause of their

3

tribulations and that it therefore lay in their own hands to win their true release.

This "saving truth" was inherited by Christianity from the prophets of Israel and "propagated in Christian guise" for the salvation of "the Hellenic World."[10] "Without this intrusion from an alien source in [of?] a principle which had already been apprehended by Syriac souls with an altogether non-Hellenic outlook, the Hellenic Society might never—even in its own 'Time of Troubles'—have succeeded in learning a lesson which was so much at variance with the dominant mood in the Hellenic Ethos." The significance of this Jewish response of the "still small voice" was then so far-reaching that without it the conversion of the Roman Empire and its peoples to Christianity might never have occurred.

Bearing this in mind one is almost tempted to the perhaps frivolous remark that, alas, the finest Time of Troubles does not last forever; and so the Syriac tribulations too came to an end with the establishment by Cyrus of an Empire that gave the Syriac world a *Pax Achaemenia*.[11] From the sixth century to the second century B.C.E. Judaism and Jewry pass through a phase of "relative stagnation."[12] No suffering, no creativity!—this is the rule. The stimulus for further growth is not again provided until the Achaemenian Empire, as the result of the conquest of Alexander the Great, is overwhelmed by the Hellenic world. And now we have a second bout of the Time of Troubles, but this time between the Syriac and the Hellenic civilizations. The conflict is narrowed down in the second century B.C.E. to one between Judaism and Hellenism—at first between Jewry and the Hellenized Syria of the Seleucids, later between Jewry and the Roman Empire, the universal state of Hellenic society. It is in this period that Judaism and the Jewish people fail miserably; it is the time of their decline and irretrievable fall.

2.

What happened to the Jewish soul after the glorious achievements of the first period of Syriac misfortune? In the opinion

4

of Mr. Toynbee, Judaism in this second Time of Troubles lapsed into militancy.[13] However, trying to analyze what that means, we come up against one of the idiosyncrasies of the profuse *Study*. The rich style is, unfortunately, not seasoned by clarity of expression; nor is the breadth of erudition controlled by consistent reasoning. The "lapse into militancy" has not remained unaffected by the author's predilection for literary luxuriance. The phrase seems to have a host of different meanings. The rebellion of the Maccabees is first described as such a lapse into militancy for the purpose of propagating a religion by methods of violence.[14] However, the record is corrected later, so as to conform more to the truth, by the admission that the Maccabees drew the sword "in self-defense, in order to save the Jewish religion from extinction."[15] This, of course, does not seem to be such a dishonorable deed, and Mr. Toynbee, in another place,[16] gives even the Pharisees a pat on the back for having supported the Maccabees in "the heroic Jewish revolt against Hellenism." But the admission is made not in order to exculpate the Maccabees but in order to pin-point their guilt. The very same sword that had been so nobly drawn was soon turned "to the new sinister use of imposing Judaism upon the neighboring non-Jewish populations . . . whom the Maccabees now succeded in bringing under their rule."[15] The reference is of course to Johanan Hyrcanus[17], who is reported by Josephus to have compelled the Idumeans to accept Judaism. The isolated action of a Hasmonean prince is construed as "the Maccabean policy of religious conversion by political force" that cost Judaism "the whole of its spiritual future."[18]

Whether the thesis makes sense or not, it means that the lapse into militancy was due to religious zeal; it had a religious motivation. This version of the "lapse" is lost sight of elsewhere in order to make room for a different one. According to another version, Jewry's struggle against Hellenism was a purely secular affair, a political enterprise with the purpose of driving an alien aggressor out of the domain of the Syriac world, a task that was later brilliantly accomplished by Islam. This then was the "disastrous aberration"—the exchanging of the religious function, proper to Judaism, for a political role. In the end

Jewry had to pay heavily "for having lent itself to a political enterprise."[19] But even this version of the "lapse" is not maintained consistently. At times Mr. Toynbee says that Judaism was perversely distracted from its "ecumenical mission of bringing human souls into a closer communion with God" and became a combatant "in the trivial mundane military enterprise of liberating a subjugated Syriac Society's domain from the incubus of an interloping Hellenic ascendancy." At times, on the other hand, Mr. Toynbee implies that the struggle between the two societies was really a *Kulturkampf* and that Judaism was deflected from its original mission and "transformed" into a weapon "of cultural warfare in the Syriac Society's retort to the Hellenic Society's aggression."[20]

And now the reader may take his choice between militancy as a policy of religious conversion, as an auxiliary in a cultural warfare, or as a struggle for political freedom. But, Mr. Toynbee himself does not make a choice; he asserts these propositions indiscriminately and simultaneously, with all their contradictory consequences.

The use of force for the conversion of souls is indeed the most monstrous perversion of religion that one can imagine. And if that was the guilt of Jewry during the period under discussion, one might even agree with the author's equation of the exploits of the "Jewish Sicarii—the 'gangsters' of the zealot persuasion"—with those of the Spanish Inquisition.[21] It is of course true that these "gangster" Zealots were fighting as soldiers, defending their homeland against the brutal military monster, whereas the Grand Inquisitors were living in the palaces of the mighty, robed in purple and satiated with power and riches, secure and safe and risking nothing of their own, wielding all the power of this world against the few and the weak who were no aggressors. Nevertheless from the point of view of the Kingdom of God, it makes little difference whether you take the sword in self-defense or as an aggressor; you will perish by the sword.[22] On the other hand, if the struggle of Jewry against Hellenism was only "a trivial mundane military enterprise" for the sake of political liberation, then it might be called foolish but not really devilish; then it does

6

make a world of difference whether you fight in self-defense, spurning life without liberty, or as an aggressor, trampling under foot the freedom and happiness of others. Surely, not even the "etherealized"[23] Mr. Toynbee would have the courage to consider all the "unsuccessful" fighters for freedom in history to be "gangsters." If Jewry's failure consisted in exchanging a religious function for a political one, then the mere mentioning of the Zealots and the Spanish Inquisition in the same breath is an unwarranted insult to the Zealots. Mr. Toynbee is perfectly right in maintaining "that the propagation of one religion at the expense of other religions through the employment of methods of barbarism, on the ground that the religion in whose name the persecution is carried on is a religion of a higher order, is a moral contradiction in terms, since oppression and injustice and cruelty are negations of the very essence of spiritual sublimity."[23] Now, this is extremely relevant in any discussion of the Inquisition; it was indeed "a moral contradiction in terms" to insist on building the Kingdom of God with "oppression and injustice and cruelty." However, the stricture does not apply to the Jewish Zealots, if theirs was a secular struggle against a secular enemy. It is certainly not a "moral contradiction" to fight on the mundane plane a mundane war of self-defense with mundane means; but it is undoubtedly the most devilish form of barbarism to "save" souls, against their own will, with iron and fire.

Similarly, the purported forcible conversion of the Idumeans ought to be re-evaluated. If Judaism was forced into a political role and the Maccabean kingdom was a purely mundane enterprise,[24] then Johanan Hyrcanus was attempting to imitate the methods of Antiochus Epiphanes, who by the brutally enforced elimination of religious diversity among his subject peoples was hoping to safeguard the political unity of his empire.[25] On this showing, Johanan Hyrcanus was doing on a small scale and in a tiny corner of the world what the conquerors of this earth did almost as a matter of political routine on a far vaster scale and with much more devastating consequences for the human race. In this case one may of course speak no longer of the "Maccabean policy of religious conversion by political force," but rather of the Machiavellian policy of all rulers—that of safeguarding the political unity of their realm at all cost, even by means of enforced religious uniformity.[26] The two concepts are incompatible.

However, inconsistency does not perturb Mr. Toynbee. Having belabored the Maccabees and the Zealots on account of their perverse policy of propagating Judaism by methods of barbarism, he proceeds lustily to reap the full harvest of his other theory that the Maccabees deserted religion for politics. But here we have to introduce another one of Mr. Toynbee's cherished concepts. What is at first called "lapse into militancy" imperceptibly merges into the ethos of violence, and we get the "antithesis between the gentle ethos of Christianity . . . and the violent ethos of Maccabean Judaism."[27] One cannot help being genuinely surprised. What happened to the "lapse" that it should deserve to be elevated to the dignity of an "ethos"? Furthermore, the lapse *into* militancy must have been a lapse *from* something else; speaking of the Maccabees, this could only have been a lapse from Judaism, which—in Mr. Toynbee's own words—in "a tremendous spiritual travail" of the first Syriac Time of Troubles had chosen the ethos of gentleness.[28] It would therefore be much more truthful, when discussing the *lapse* of the Maccabees from the religion of their fathers, to speak of the antithesis between the gentle ethos of Judaism and the violent ethos of the Maccabees.

For an unbiased mind, however, the most puzzling point here is the phrase "Maccabean Judaism." In fact, there is no such things and there never was. The Maccabees were neither teachers nor interpreters of Judaism. In matters of religion they were followers and not leaders. Yet the term is a cornerstone in the structure of Mr. Toynbee. From the point of view of a Higher Religion the lapse into militancy is a grave aberration; but a sin that affects the soul of the sinner still leaves untainted the purity of his religion. An undespoiled Judaism, however, will never satisfy Mr. Toynbee. Accordingly, the Maccabees are said to have deserted the religious plane of life for a political one, thus transforming Judaism itself; they created a Judaism of their own, a kind of mundane religion. For the political task of liberating a society under physical assault, militancy is the only possible way of action; indeed, it is a virtue, the ethos of a mundane civilization. What we have is no longer a "lapse," but "a change of ethos";[29] and since this changes the very essence of a religion, we get "the violent ethos of Maccabean Judaism."

It should not be difficult to guess how the other Judaism, the good one, the higher religion of the prophets of Israel, has been whisked away from the scene of history. This is how Mr. Toynbee puts it:

> After the *transformation* of Judaism and Zoroastrianism into instruments of Syriac political opposition to a Hellenic dominant minority, the Syriac religious genius took refuge among those elements in the Syriac population under Hellenic ascendancy which were reacting to the challenge in the gentle and not in the violent way; and, in giving birth to Christianity and Mithraism as its contributions to the spiritual travail of a Hellenic internal proletariat, Syriac religion found new expressions for a spirit and an outlook which Judaism and Zoroastrianism had repudiated.[30]

This statement neatly condenses most of the terminology of the *Study,* and no doubt has a certain dignity of its own. Attempting to translate it into plain English, by leaving out all references to Zoroastrianism and Mithraism[31] (and therefore reading for "Syriac religious" and "Syriac religion," "Jewish religious" and "Jewish religion"), and by equating "the gentle and not violent way" with the way of the original Judaism that was "transformed," we can perhaps maintain that what Mr. Toynbee says is this: After the transformation of Judaism into an instrument of Syriac political opposition to Hellenic domination, the Jewish religious genius took refuge among those people who reacted to the challenge in the Jewish way; and, in giving birth to Christianity, Jewish religion found a new expression (meaning Christianity) for a spirit and an outlook (meaning Judaism) which Judaism had repudiated. Now, even though he says so, Mr. Toynbee does not really mean that Judaism repudiated Judaism; that would be silly. The

9

unfortunate impression arises from the fact that "Judaism" and "Jewish" are used in two different ways in the same sentence. Almost throughout the entire sentence the words stand for their original "pre-transformation" meaning; only once, in the final clause, is "Judaism" used in the sense which it received after its "transformation." It was this "transformed" Judaism that repudiated the classical Judaism of Israel. Classical Judaism "found new expressions" in Christianity, when—as the result of the rather illegitimate birth of Maccabean Judaism—the Jewish spiritual genius (the classical one!) took refuge outside a faithless Jewry. The Judaism of the prophets having been taken over by Christianity, the "antithesis" is now between the gentle ethos of Christianity and the violent ethos of Maccabean Judaism. The Judaism which Jewry itself is permitted to retain for its own use is the "transformed" Judaism of the Maccabees; and, since no other remains, Mr. Toynbee proceeds to drop the adjective "Maccabean" and speak boldly of the violent ethos of Judaism.

The idea is neither very original nor very exciting. We seem to have heard before that the real Jews, in the classical sense of the word, are the Gentiles, and the real Gentiles the Jews. New and original is only the way Mr. Toynbee develops this hoary theme of anti-Jewish conceit. However, let us not allow him to confuse us. When he speaks of the violent ethos of Judaism, he can only mean this new-fangled, "transformed," political Judaism, which according to him was a Maccabean creation and which, in *his* view, is the religion of Jewry.

The idea of the "lapse into militancy," on the other hand, must not be confused with the "violent ethos"; it does not refer to the "transformed" Judaism but, on the contrary, makes sense only from the viewpoint of the classical Judaism of the prophets. If the Maccabean policy was "religious conversion by political force," then there was "lapse into militancy" but no "transformation" of Judaism—and therefore no "change of ethos" either. Unfortunately, Mr. Toynbee does not indicate any awareness that these two concepts are mutually exclusive. As we have already seen—and as we shall observe yet more closely—he treats them as if they were interchangeable. Finally, let us keep in mind the point, so eloquently made by Mr. Toynbee, that in Christianity "untransformed" Judaism "found new expressions." Nor let us overlook the not altogether unimportant matter that when Mr. Toynbee speaks of the gentle ethos of Christianity, the term includes the gentle ethos of Judaism, "inherited from the Prophets of Israel."[32] He rightly calls it Christian in contradistinction to "Jewish" only in accordance with the meaning that the word "Jewish" acquires within his *own* construction and as a result of but one of his interpretations of the Maccabean performance.

3.

The question that still must be answered is: How could a people, or a religion, that started out so promisingly fall so low? What was the reason for "the unfortunate change of ethos" or turn to violence? According to Mr. Toynbee, Jewry's stumbling block was its immature Messianic idea. Jewish Messianism meant the restoration of "the fallen national kingdom at some hidden future date."[33] Although such an expectation does mean a turning away from the external world, it is not the "transference of action from the Macrocosm to the Microcosm," which we have recognized as the secret of the successful response to a challenge; it is not a genuine spiritual withdrawal from the world. Though the Jewish Messianic expectations were directed toward the future, they were awaiting a realm that was not essentially different from the existing one, but only more pleasant for Jewry. Such a concept of "the Kingdom" is an "external Utopia," which "is intended to do duty, in place of the inward spiritual cosmos, as an 'Other World'; but it is 'Other World' only in the shallow and unsatisfying sense of being a negation of the Macrocosm in the momentary present of the Macrocosm's existence here and now."[34] Jewish Messianism may, therefore, best be called Futurism; it is the attempt to solve the problem of a society in a state of disintegration by a mere external change in the time-dimension. It is true that for several centuries after the fall of Jerusalem to Nebuchadnezzar, Jewish Messianism did work "in favour of gentleness," and we see how the early martyrs in Judaism's struggle with Hellenism gave their lives without offering any physical resistance. Yet, Futurism is bound to fail. The strain between "a confidently expected mundane future and an excruciatingly experienced mundane present" becomes unbearable and is resolved "in violence in the end." And so we find that the "martyrdom of Eleazar and the Seven Brethren was followed, within two years, by the armed insurrection of Judas Maccabaeus." This opened the era "of ever more fanatically militant Jewish Zealots ... whose violence reached its appalling climax in the Satanic Jewish *emeutes* of . . . 66-70 and 115-17 and 132-5" of the c.e.[35]

The answer to the problem of Jewry should have been Transfiguration, which differs from Futurism in that it represents "a genuine change in spiritual clime" and not "a mere transfer in the Time-dimension."[36] It seems to imply a transformation of human nature, a kind of "awakening of the soul to the presence," a rejection of this mundane world and the discovery of the Kingdom of God. It was the ultimately triumphant answer of Jesus "whose servants were forbidden to fight because his Kingdom was not of this World." Jewry could not accept such a solution since the Kingdom of God brought salvation to all mankind, whereas the Jews awaited it only for themselves as God's Chosen People. This is what Mr. Toynbee calls the "idolization of an ephemeral self," the fateful error for which "the most notorious historical example" are the Jews. It is the Nemesis of Creativity in Jewry; indeed, the end of all further Jewish creativity. Having risen high above their contemporaries in the first phase of the Syriac Time of Troubles by the discovery of an omnipresent and omnipotent God, "they allowed themselves to be captivated by a temporary and relative half-truth. They persuaded themselves that Israel's discovery of the One True God had revealed Israel itself to be God's Chosen People; and this half-truth inveigled them into the fatal error of looking upon a momentary spiritual eminence, which they had attained by labour and travail, as a privilege conferred upon them by God in a covenant which was everlasting."[37] In such sinful self-delusion the Jews "rested on their oars" when

12

the crisis of the impact of Hellenism upon the Syriac Society challenged them to a renewed creative response. "By persisting in this posture, they 'put themselves out of the running' for serving once more as pioneers in the next advance of the Syriac spirit."[37] They were unable to recognize "the true fulfillment of Jewry's long cherished Messianic Hope"[38] when it was granted to them in the person of Jesus. Thus Jewry went down to perdition.

It is somewhat amusing to find that with all the accouterments of modern historic research Mr. Toynbee could not uncover more than the homely old Christian commonplace that Jewry was punished forever for its rejection of Jesus. Of course, being an eminently enlightened *post-Christian Christian*,[39] he will not say that Jewry was punished by a direct Act of God, as it were, to testify through its eternal wanderings to its own perfidy. Things do not happen that way in history. There are laws and there is a pattern, like the Nemesis of Creativity and the inevitable failure of Futurism. However, since Mr. Toynbee perceives "in History a vision of God's creation on the move"[40] there is not really much difference between an Act of God and the Laws of History, which are also of God—except that a Law is always more inexorable than an Act of Will. Whereas according to the old dispensation Jews "have wandered about, regarded as an accursed race, as an object of contempt to other peoples,"[41] in the opinion of Mr. Toynbee they got entangled with the Laws of History and, as might be expected, were crushed completely and forever. The "accursed race" is still alive and there may be some hope for it; but of what is crushed by the mills of God, so ingeniously built into the workings of history, only "debris" or "pulverized social ash" remains.[42] Judaism and Jewry look as if they were alive; actually they are the fossilized remnants "of the extinct Syriac Society in the particular phase of disintegration in which that Society happened to find itself at the moment when it was smitten by the impact of Hellenism in the fourth century" of the C.E.[43]

For the sake of clarity, however, let us establish the fact that if the ultimate fall of Jewry consisted in the rejection of the "Jewish Messiah" who was offered to Jewry by the One True

God, then what Mr. Toynbee says about Jewish Messianism being identical with Futurism is rather confusing. Since, in his own view, Jesus represented "the true fulfillment of Jewry's long cherished Messianic Hope," it is obvious that the true meaning of those hopes could not have meant merely the reestablishment of "the fallen national kingdom at some hidden future date." Whatever Jewish Messianism be, on Mr. Toynbee's own admission it is not what he says it is—a leap in the time-dimension toward a mundane Jewish national paradise. What he possibly has in mind when he discusses the nature of Jewish Messianism is not the proper philosophical or theological term, but the purely empirical idea. Mr. Toynbee assumes that the Jews of the Maccabean period understood by Messianism nothing but a mundane national restoration. This would then be the counterpart to Mr. Toynbee's discovery of Maccabean Judaism; a "transformed" Jewish Messianism, eminently becoming to a "transformed" Judaism. What we shall have to ascertain is: Who did the transforming—Maccabean Jewry or Mr. Toynbee?

2. JUDAISM AS A TRIBAL RELIGION AND JEWRY'S DREAM OF WORLD DOMINION

1.

It would appear that between writing Volume V and Volume VI of his *Study,* Mr. Toynbee did some more thinking on the subject of Jewish Messianism and, to his great dismay, must have discovered that his interpretation of it as a mundane hope for a mundane national kingdom was not at all convincing.

Just imagine what a mundane Messiah would have to accomplish. After the fall of their country, the Jews were dispersed over the world. The Messiah would have to lead them out of their world-wide exile and reunite them in their national kingdom. Unfortunately between the hope and its realization there stood the might of the Great King and, at a later date, that of the Caesars. It is fairly obvious that, since—according to the premise—the restoration was to be a purely mundane undertaking, the mundane world-powers of the day would also have had some say in the matter, which of course would have complicated things somewhat. The Jewish people were shattered and scattered; the two "puny, ephemeral principalities" that had once been their homeland were effectively incorporated as minor provinces—or parts of provinces—in a vast all-powerful universal state. What madness could have moved a completely fragmentized and impotent Jewry to expect to wrest their mundane liberation by mundane means from the mailed fist of omnipotent Empire? In terms of the mundane world, within which a mundane Jewish Messianism was supposed to operate, what Mr. Toynbee said on the subject must be deemed hopeless bunkum.

However, a historian like Mr. Toynbee is never at a loss to save his theories by buttressing them with new ones. Jewry realized well enough that as long as the might of the Great King or of Caesar remained unimpaired they would have no chance of liberating themselves from the foreign yoke. Well, that was just too bad for a Cyrus, or a Titus, or a Hadrian; they would have to go. At first, one would try to use diplomacy; if it did not work, *nolens volens,* one would have to use force. Now, is this not most ingenious! Those old Jews were no fools; that is what Mr. Toynbee says. He recognizes that

> ... if the New David was effectively to reunite all Jewry under his rule—and what but this was his mission?—in an age, in which the living generation of Jews was scattered over the face of the Earth, then he must gird himself to acquire a dominion to which his forebears had never aspired in the highest flights of their ambition. He must wrest the sceptre of *world-empire* from the hands of its present holder and must make Jerusalem become tomorrow what Susa was today and what Babylon had been yesterday. In order to reunite the Jews he must now reign as King of Kings over Jews and Gentiles alike. And why, after all, should the coming champion of Jewry not attain this pinnacle of power and glory? In a world in which a Cyrus or Seleucus could rise and a Cambyses or Anti-

ochus the Great could fall with the speed of lightning when it flickers between the Earth and the Firmament, why should not a Zerubbabel have as good a chance of world dominion as a Darius, or a Judas Maccabaeus as an Antiochus Epiphanes, or a Bar Kokaba as a Hadrian?"[44]

Mr. Toynbee's boldness of vision is at times breath-taking. However, should anyone doubt its basic soundness, let him turn to Volume V, pp. 412-19 of the *Study,* where in a philosophical dissertation our author himself has already proved that "the belief in the omnipotence of Chance . . . is apt to prevail in times of social disintegration."

Having conceived the policy of world dominion, the Jews proceeded to implement it. There was, for instance, "Deutero-Isaiah," who hailed Cyrus as the Lord's anointed "in the wild hope that the Persian conqueror may be moved to bestow his world-empire upon the Jews!"[45] Then there were the short-lived successes of Zerubbabel and of the Maccabees, both having in common the purpose of providing "a nucleus for the Messianic Empire that was shortly to be expected."[46] It was not until Jewry was completely crushed in the appalling insurrections against omnipotent Rome that in the final rebellion of Bar Kokba "the hope of a new mundane Jewish commonwealth was finally extinguished."[47] It had taken the Jews from about 522 B.C.E. to 135 C.E. "to learn by an agonizing process of trial and error that Futurism simply would not work."

2.

Having reached this point in our deliberations, we are now introduced to the rather startling revelation that in "the bankruptcy of Futurism the Jews made the further tremendous discovery of the existence of the Kingdom of God."[48] In order to be able to follow Mr. Toynbee in his development of this theme, we must perform a deed of intellectual acrobatics and erase from our memory what we heard from our author about the development of Judaism as a Higher Religion. Did he not say that the "fable of Solomon's Choice is a parable of the history of the Chosen People," whose first concern was the search

16

for the Kingdom of God, that the greatest achievement of that early Syriac civilization was its discovery of the particular conception of God which is common to Judaism, Zoroastrianism, Christianity, and Islam? Did he not declare that the first Syriac Time of Troubles, beginning with the Assyrian conquests and ending by the establishment of the Achaemenian Empire, was the period of Syriac creativity, in that during this period the prophets of Israel developed an "embryonic Higher Religion" into a mature one? Did Mr. Toynbee not maintain that monotheistic Judaism was "the positive and immense spiritual achievement of the Prophets of Israel and Judah?"[49] All this must now be treated as if it had never been mentioned; that is how Mr. Toynbee himself treats in this part of his *Study* what he himself has thus far said about Judaism as a Higher Religion.

Now, the period of creativity begins with the establishment of the Achaemenian Empire, which ushered in a time that was previously described as a phase of stagnation.[50] We are now asked to believe that the pre-exilic prophets of Israel—Hosea, Amos, Isaiah, Jeremiah, and the others—had no inkling of the One True God. In their eyes "the victory of the Assyrians and Chaldeans over the prophets' countrymen is the work of the victim's own national god . . ."[51] Thus spoke that Teutonic scholar Eduard Meyer, whose work has now become Mr. Toynbee's Holy Bible on Judaism. The purification of this parochial concept started only with the creation of the Achaemenian Empire in 525 B.C.E. In the law and order of the universal state of the Syriac civilization the petty subject people from the hills of Judea beheld for the first time the image of a *universal* law and a *universal* order; and behind it all they could not help perceiving the *likeness* of a universal ruler, namely that of the Achaemenian Great King. This new experience released a process of religious fermentation, and under "the influence of the Achaemenian Monarchy upon the Jewish conception of the God of Israel" Jewry was led toward the idea of a "Unique and Omnipotent God."[52] But, although the vision of a universal ruler in human shape started off this phase of religious growth, by itself it would apparently not have been

17

potent enough to bring about the culmination of the new development. As always, trouble was needed as a stimulus. This duly set in with the collapse of the Achaemenian universal state under the impetus of the conquests of Alexander the Great. This new Time of Troubles, by bringing about the final defeat of Futurism, is mainly responsible for the emergence of the Jewish faith in an omnipotent and righteous God.

It was the "mundane situation," not at all favorable to the Jews and continually deteriorating, which compelled Jewry to revise its concept of a protecting national divinity. After all, as we may still remember, the Jews "had set their hands to a task which was, *humanly speaking,* an impossible one; for, when they had failed to preserve their independence, how could they rationally hope to reconquer it—and, what is more, to supplant their own conquerors in the lordship of the World —by the strength of their own right arm?"[53] The question has, of course, already been answered once: they started out in their plans for world dominion with the "belief in the omnipotence of Chance." One must therefore assume that the Jewish faith in Chance just helped Jewry to conceive the idea of world empire but, as might have been expected, was unable to survive the disappointments of the first Jewish defeats. At that point, one must again assume, the Jews could have done the very reasonable thing and given up their idiotic hankering after world conquest. Fortunately for them and the rest of mankind, being the "stiff-necked" people that they have always been, rather than give up the wild dream of empire they remembered their old god "from the uplands"—he must have lived in semi-retirement during the short sway of the goddess Chance—and began "the widening of the conception of the protecting divinity." The Jewish ambition, having waxed world-embracing, proceeded to equip the tribal deity with sufficient power to guarantee world-wide fulfillment.

To succeed in this tremendous undertaking they must have behind them a god who was not only competent to see fair play but was also capable of redressing a balance that, on any human reckoning, was hopelessly inclined

18

against this god's terrestrial protégés. If the protégés were engaged on a forlorn hope, then the protector must be nothing less than omnipotent—and it would follow from this that he must also be actively and whole-heartedly righteous; for only an all-powerful godhead who cared for righteousness above everything else would be both able and willing to exert himself with effect on behalf of a people whose cause was just but whose worldly position was insignificant.[54]

With one big leap from the parochial domain of "a barbarous" tribal deity, we have landed in the Kingdom of an omnipotent and righteous God or—rather—god. Actually, "Yahweh did not cease to be thought of as the parochial god of Jewry in a certain sense." In view of "the mundane situation" it had to be an omnipotent and righteous "divinity who stood behind the devoted human leader of a futurist forlorn hope." As Futurism fails, the human figure fades away, "while the divinity who has originally been called in aid merely in order to give supernatural power to the human elbow of 'the Lord's Anointed' now comes to dominate the scene." Thus, by bitter experience Jewry learns that "a human Messiah is not enough. God himself must condescend to play the part, which He alone can effectively play, of serving His people as their saviour and their king."[55]

This, of course, is neither history nor theology but psychology: a psychological explanation of how the idea of an omnipotent Godhead developed in the minds of Jewry, which says nothing about the objective existence of the Godhead. Jewry formed the concept of a god in the image of its needs. Mr. Toynbee cannot overlook the fact that he has described the progress of escapism with which modern psychoanalysis is so familiar: an unhappy people that set itself an unattainable goal imposes the responsibility of action upon a whole series of substitutes. First it is a human champion; when he fails, he is fortified by the backing of an imaginary divinity; "and finally, when even the Lord's Anointed breaks down, the fools in desperation signal S.O.S. to a wholly fictitious divine being whose alleged omnipotence is expected to make up for the proven impotence of his human inventors." Mr. Toynbee believes that this may have been true of the militant Zealots and the pacifist Quietists among the Jews. The first were convinced that their God would take upon Himself the fulfillment of their "self-appointed mundane task," whereas the latter refrained from all action in the faith that the realization of their mundane dream was God's own concern. That was still Futurism. There were, however, two other answers—those of Rabbi Johanan ben Zakkai and of the Christian Church. The psychoanalytical diagnosis does not apply to them, since the very essence of their response was the surrendering of the foolish goal of Futurism, "a withdrawal of the *libido* from the previous mundane aim." Surrendering the purpose of Futurism, they put their treasure "in a purpose which is not Man's but God's and which therefore can only be pursued in a spiritual field of supra-mundane dimensions."[56]

3.

The intriguing aspect of this theory is that the concept of a god, which was originally a mere figment of escapism, turned out to correspond to the One True God of the Universe. The bankruptcy of Futurism was like the rending of the veil of the Temple, which revealed the reality of an Other World that was always present but unseen or unrecognized. Most surprising of all, however, is the revelation that only now is the One True God discovered in this "spiritual reorientation"—the discoverers being Rabbi Johanan ben Zakkai on the one hand and the Christian Church on the other. In this psychological interpretation of Judaism, Mr. Toynbee proceeds as if David and Solomon, Elijah and Elisha, Hosea, Amos, Micah, Isaiah and Jeremiah, Hillel and the other prophets, teachers, leaders, and saints of Israel had never lived. It is obvious that our author has become the victim of his own fabrications. Having decided that Jewish Messianism wanted nothing but a mundane national kingdom, he could not suppress that very logical question, how —according to the Jews—such a task was to be accomplished.

Having then answered, rather cleverly, that the only solution to the problem of Jewish political and military helplessness was Jewish world dominion, to be initiated with the propitious assistance of Omnipotent Chance, he was inevitably led on to the discovery of "the rake's progress in escapism." It was rather logical to expect—was it not?—that a people as broken and scattered as the Jews were, had it believed in the One True God, would have turned to Him for help in a contrite spirit and with a longing heart—exactly as described in Mr. Toynbee's original version of Judaism, but now denied— rather than seeking their salvation in a mad mundane ambition for world conquest. One must therefore begin with a tribal deity, whose power is weakly, and rather narrowly, circumscribed, and call in the Goddess Chance to start escapism rolling by way of Futurism into the ante chamber of "the Kingdom." Of course, there might have been no need for such an imaginative reconstruction of Judaism and Jewish history, had Mr. Toynbee assumed that Jewish Messianism was not quite so mundane, that the Maccabees—notwithstanding their numerous shortcomings—did not "transform" Judaism into a mere instrument of political struggle with world empires. His impressions of Judaism and Jewry might have been very much different, had he allowed the Jewish hopes for a return to Zion to be in some way related to a Jewish faith in the One God, had he granted them at least some "other worldly," religious significance. But this is exactly what he cannot do—let go of the idea of a mundane Jewish Messianism. We shall have to understand why the concept is so dear to him.

In the meantime, however, let us note the significance of this theory in its relationship to the first presentation of Judaism as a Higher Religion. Originally, the sense of sin played an important part in leading Jewry to the discovery of an "Other World of supra-mundane dimensions" and to a closer communion with the One True God; now,[57] on the contrary, it is a sense of self-righteousness, the conviction of the people that their "cause was just," which produces the concept of an omnipotent and righteous God. Futurism, which meant desertion from the presence of God, now—of intrinsic escapist necessity—equips itself with a faith that brings Jewry much closer to the One God than they had ever been before. On this showing, one can no longer speak of a "Nemesis of Creativity," upon which earlier Jewry's downfall was blamed.[58] On the contrary, one must now assume that there was a continuous growth from the post-exilic tribal deity to Futurism and, through Futurism, to Transfiguration in its rabbinical (represented by Rabbi Johanan ben Zakkai!) and Judeo-Christian variations. Mr. Toynbee has now every reason to be grateful to the sin of Jewish Futurism. Without this Jewry would have submitted to its fate and would have certainly disappeared in the universal melting pots of the Achaemenian and Romano-Hellenic empires, like all its other contemporaries. There might never have occurred "the renting of the veil in the Temple," and one would have to write a study of history regarding "the true end of man" from the standpoint of "a Syriac Mithras, an Egyptian Isis, a Hittite Cybele."[59]

In the following pages, for the sake of brevity, we shall often refer to Toynbee's first version of the full development of Judaism in the prophetic age as the "theological" one. The second version, in which the role of the prophets of Israel and Judah is completely ignored, and the motivating force of development is the Jewish escapism of the period from 525 B.C.E. to 70 C.E., we shall call the "psychological" one.

3. JUDAISM AS CHRISTIANITY'S "ORIGINAL" SIN

1.

Parallel to the psychological version of Judaism we are also given an interpretation of Christianity, which seems to be required by the new understanding. In the sixth volume of the *Study,* one finds a very elaborate discussion of the points of difference between Judaism and Christianity as they became manifest in the personality of Jesus.

Mr. Toynbee dwells on "the direct influence of the Hellenic motif" on the Christian presentation of the story of the birth of Jesus. Quoting from E. Meyer's *Ursprung und Anfaenge des Christentums,* Mr. Toynbee underscores "the correspondence between Matthew and the legend of the birth of Plato," which is "as exact as it could possibly be." There are at least six Hellenic stories of the same nature on record, and if we "compare the birth-story of Jesus with that of Herakles, we shall find a still greater number of points of correspondence than Meyer has pointed out in his comparison of the birth-story of Jesus with that of Plato." Mr. Toynbee insists that "to a Jewish mind the Christian attribution of a divine paternity to Jesus seems like a lapse from the slowly and painfully attained monotheism of the Chosen People of the One True God into one of the grossest and most unedifying superstitions of a Hellenic paganism."

The other even more fundamental difference between Judaism and Christianity is that according to the Jewish view the Messianic King is a purely human being, "The Anointed of the Lord," invested by Him with authority; whereas in Christian opinion he is God Incarnate, "the King of God's Kingdom—and a King who is God Himself and not God's less-than-divine deputy."[60] And again Mr. Toynbee rightly points out that concepts of a god incarnate and of a dying god are quite well known to Hellenic and other forms of paganism but have no place whatsoever in Judaism. A Jewish reader is somewhat astounded by the amount of scholarship and literary energy that the author spends on proving something that is part of the A B C of Judaism, until the reader realizes that the laborious and long-winded discussion is addressed to Toynbee's own fellow Christians, who—regrettably—overlook what is rather "notorious," namely, that "the view that the Messiah has to be born of a virgin is . . . quite unknown to the Jews." Mr. Toynbee is most anxious to impress upon them the influence of the pagan and—in particular—Hellenic motifs. The importance of these religious influences from paganism is underlined by the fact that in the figure of "Divus Augustus the potential converts of the first Christian missionaries had already acknowledged an incarnation of the Godhead in a living human being whose mortal mother was fabled to have been got with child by an immortal sire. . . ." Understandably, the happy coincidence of such preparation of souls must have rendered

23

the task of the missionaries very much easier. Truly significant, however, is the use Mr. Toynbee makes of the Hellenic influence. He maintains that "the Christian evolutionist's inference from this would be, not that there was no truth in Christianity, but that the truth which was in Christianity had already been aglow in paganism for ages before it had burst into a Christian plane."[61] In other words, the truth that is the very essence of the Christian message was known to the heathens in a less intense form even before the Christian epiphany, and there is a sort of evolutionary continuity between that message in its pagan manifestation and its fuller exposition in Christianity.

We shall have no quarrel with Mr. Toynbee over his interpretation of Christianity. From the standpoint of our analysis of his ideas, however, we cannot help observing that "the direct influence of the Hellenic motif" is—in other passages—complemented by what may perhaps be called the indirect influence of Jesus' Gentile descent. The "Messiah of Jewry," says Mr. Toynbee, "comes out of that obscure village in 'Galilee of the Gentiles' "; he is the "inspired Jewish scion of forcibly converted Galilean Gentiles"; or, as he is also referred to, he is Jewry's "Galilean step-child."[62] In short, the truth of Jesus' divine parentage was "aglow in paganism for ages" before its fuller revelation in the Christian garb, and the potential of his human parentage lay dormant, as it were, in the womb of Galilean Gentiledom for ages before its materialization in the Jewish frame. In order to grasp better the trend of the author's thoughts, one must remember that Mr. Toynbee also maintains that as to the vital concept of the unity of mankind the source of "the human inspiration in the mind of Jesus" was the "Alexandrian vision" of that idea. The spirit of Alexander the Great was "in the air" in Palestine. This again is what one would expect to hear from Mr. Toynbee. The unity of mankind is the corollary to the fatherhood of God. Alexander did entertain that notion, but Jewry did not. After all, a God who is jealous and intolerant, who "never ceased to be thought of as the parochial god of Jewry," who is Power and not Love, could not be expected to promote the idea of the brotherhood of men.[63]

24

It is true, Mr. Toynbee does not make Jesus a Galilean Aryan, as is customary in Teutonic theological "research"; but he has certainly de-judaized him thoroughly. It would seem that the only connection that "Jewry's Messiah" has with Judaism is his complete break with it; and one may even wonder what could be meant by "the Galilean Jewish prophet whose message to his fellow men was the consummation of all previous Jewish experience."[64] What that message seems now—i.e., in Volume VI—to consummate more than anything else is a great deal of pagan, Hellenic, and Alexandrine vision and experience. Mr. Toynbee wishes to make the point that, beside Judaism, the other "tributary" of Christianity was Hellenism; and he makes the point so successfully that his acknowledgment of "the immensity of this Jewish empire in the spiritual dimension," neatly tucked away in an annex to Volume VI, sounds hollow, a mere hypocritical lip service to the traditional Christian belief "that the coming of Christ is the fulfillment of Scripture."[65] His efforts to separate Christianity from Judaism are the logical consequences of his psychological version of the development of Judaism. The relationship between the two religions was, at first, according to the theological interpretation, indicated unequivocally. After the "transformation" of Judaism by Maccabean and Zealot Jewry, the Jewish religious genius took refuge among those segments of the internal proletariat of the Hellenic world that remained loyal to the spirit of the "untransformed" Judaism and, in bringing Christianity forth, gave a new expression to that spirit.[66] This did make sense as long as Judaism was described as a Higher Religion which in the creative travail of the prophets of Israel and Judah found its majestic manifestation as an ecumenical faith; it does not make sense in relation to a parochial religion, to which Judaism has now been reduced. A tribal deity who through the unexpected luck of a psychological aberration "widens" into an omnipotent and universal god, but who remains chained to its tribal past, is nothing much to be proud about; the separation of Christianity from such a Judaism becomes an intrinsic necessity.

25

2.

Does Mr. Toynbee, by producing his psychological version of Judaism, mean to repudiate his original theological version? We have already seen that he is not perturbed by the inconsistency of his various theories as long as he can make each of them consistent within itself. He holds on to both of his versions of Judaism, just as we saw him hold on simultaneously to his contradictory interpretations of Maccabean history.[67] His method of using mutually exclusive theories is strikingly illustrated by the final interpretation he places on the Maccabean guilt of Jewry and the significance he attaches to it.

Discussing the various forms of "Encounters Between Civilizations," Mr. Toynbee also surveys anti-Semitism. In this connection he deals with the persecution of Jewry by the Visigoths, who placed before them the choice of either accepting Christianity or banishment from the country. In this kind of persecution of the Jews he is able to discern "a hidden vein of tragic irony," for—believe it or not—the first people in history to indulge in such a barbarous misuse of power against a minority were the Jews themselves. Says our author:

> The earliest known instance of 'bigotry' [Toynbee's play on the possible etymological derivation of the term from 'Visigoth'!] is the compulsory conversion of the conquered Gentiles of Galilee to Judaism by their Maccabean Jewish conqueror Alexander Jannaeus[68] . . . and the Maccabean temper was inherited by Christendom from a Jewry that came to be the principal victim of this Jewish vein in the Christian religion. Jewish "Maccabeanism" was not, of course, the sole source of Christian "Antisemitism" . . . but the combination of a fanatical religious intolerance with an antipathy arising from social and economic grievances was an aggravation of pre-Christian "Antisemitism" into which Christianity was betrayed by the Judaic, not the Hellenic, element in its ethos.[69]

Having recovered from the first impact of the Toynbean sledge hammer, a Jew is grateful to find that the "Judaic" responsibility for the crimes of Christian anti-Semitism is not really meant to be as grievous as he at first gathered. Mr. Toynbee does concede that the "Jewish vein in the Christian religion" is not the only possible cause of anti-Semitism. As is well known, there was anti-Semitism in the Hellenic world,— a fact dramatically exemplified by the persecutions and pogroms in Alexandria at the time of Philo. Undoubtedly, it could not have originated from a non-existent "Judaic element" in the Hellenic ethos. What Mr. Toynbee wishes to explain is the specific Christian anti-Semitism, which—as he well realizes —has been so much more sordid and inhuman than the pre-Christian anti-Semitism of the heathens. On this he maintains that the Christian form of anti-Semitism is an aggravation of the anti-Semitic infection, which was already acute when Christianity first appeared on the scene and which—one guesses —Christianity "inherited" from its Hellenic "tributary". In other words, if, for the sake of clarity, one wished to express it in the form of an equation, one would have to say: Christian Anti-Semitism = Pre-Christian, Hellenic Anti-Semitism + An Aggravation. However, An Aggravation = A Fanatical Religious Intolerance (alias Maccabean Temper) + An Antipathy. Therefore one might also say: Christian Anti-Semitism = Hellenic Anti-Semitism + Maccabean Temper + An Antipathy. For the Hellenic component no doubt only the Hellenic element in the Christian ethos can be blamed; for the Maccabean temper the blame is placed on the Judaic element; to whom the "antipathy arising from social and economic grievances" is to be charged is not stated. The Christian element in the Christian ethos bears no responsibility whatever; one can only guess that, being outmatched by a majority of at least two to one, its effectiveness is neutralized. Bearing in mind the feats of Hellenic anti-Semitism and pondering over the potentialities for persecution that are extant in an antipathy of the kind here described, it is rather difficult to put out of one's mind the thought that had there never been a Maccabean temper for Christendom to inherit the story of Christian Anti-semitism would still be a far more "sordid tale" than that of the pre-Christian brand.

Let us now analyze Mr. Toynbee's reasoning about the boomerang action of the "Judaic element" in the Christian ethos. He does not suggest that the Visigoths merely imitated the religious intolerance of the Maccabees. It is unlikely that they knew much about the religious policy of the one or two petty "Maccabean" (i.e. Hasmonean) princes in question, which found some vague recording in a few words of the Jewish historian Josephus. It would indeed be silly to suggest that one or two obscure incidents of Hasmonean history could have inspired with a barbarous fanaticism the Visigoths of the Iberian peninsula to enact the same kind of policy seven or eight centuries later. What Mr. Toynbee suggests is that the Maccabean temper became a constituent part of Christianity— "this Jewish vein in the Christian religion." But by itself such a pronouncement is hardly convincing. A religion, we assume, is a set of dogmas, beliefs, and values, which is consciously embraced; a temper, on the other hand, is a not-very-pleasant propensity of human nature. How on earth can a temper be so "inherited" that it becomes the constituent part of a religion! And so, as if to smooth out the wrinkles on a reader's forehead, in the next sentence Mr. Toynbee paraphrases "the Maccabean temper" by "Maccabeanism." An "ism" is much more dignified than a mere temper; an "ism" has an ideology. Since, however, "Maccabeanism" is—in the same sentence— supplanted by "a fanatical religious intolerance," which is like a reversion to the Maccabean temper, one must assume that both the temper and the intolerance are an "ism" because they represent a consciously adopted attitude which was suggested by a principle of Judaism. This then is the "Judaic element" in the Christian ethos: not a mere temper, nor just intolerance, but part of an ideology. Something of the very ethos of Judaism got into Christianity and rebounded against the Jews. And so we have rediscovered our old friend, "the violent ethos of Maccabean Judaism."[70]

It is nevertheless unusual for an experienced author like Mr. Toynbee to use the term "temper" as if it were an ideology, and to use the subjective emotional disturbance of fanatical intolerance to indicate an ethos. Nor does he do it unintentionally. He needs both the Maccabean temper and the Maccabean "ism." The two terms are purposefully left vague and made to mean practically the same thing. Going out to prove what he wants to prove, Mr. Toynbee is in a quandary. Did he not say that, when the Maccabees "transformed" the Judaism of the prophetic age into a political instrument to be used for a mundane purpose and thus effected "the unfortunate change of ethos" in Judaism from gentleness to militancy, the religious genius of the Judaism of gentleness found its new expression in the Christian garb? Did he not also declare that, as the result of that event, the violent ethos of Maccabean Judaism was *the antithesis* to the gentle ethos of Christianity?[71] All this, of course, means that there is no connection whatever between "Maccabeanism" and Christianity, and that the Judaic element in the Christian ethos is inherited from the classical Judaism of the way of gentleness, which was repudiated by "Maccabeanism." Yet, at the same time, we remember that there was another version of the Maccabean misdeeds. According to this, the Maccabees were not engaged in a petty mundane enterprise and did not "transform" Judaism into a political weapon. On the contrary, inspired by zeal for the religion of their fathers, they conceived "a policy of religious conversion by political force." Obviously, only this version of the Maccabean policy may be dubbed "bigotry" and compared to the religious policies of the Visigoths. This version may yield a Maccabean *lapse* from Judaism into militancy, a Maccabean sin or temper, but no new Maccabean Judaism with a changed ethos.[72] The Judaism of the Maccabees with a temper of religious intolerance is the same Judaism of gentleness that was taken over by Christianity.

This then is the dilemma: The mundane Maccabean "ism" has an ethos of violence but, far from being a Judaic element in Christianity, it is its antithesis; the Maccabean temper of the "religious" version does have some contact with Christendom, both having the same Judaism of the prophetic age for their religious background, but it provides no Judaic element of violence for the ethos of Christianity. Mr. Toynbee is not overwhelmed by logical difficulties of this kind. He lets the

event of the conversion of some Gentiles by the Maccabees fulfill a double function. Its religious interpretation gave us the
"Maccabean temper"; from the mundane one followed the
Maccabean "ism." Though they are exclusive of each other,
they are put to work together. What one cannot do, will be
accomplished by the other. All that is needed is vagueness and
ambiguity—and the boomerang effect of the Maccabean policy
will sound plausible. The recipe is ingenious: Take Maccabean
temper, Maccabeanism, a fanatic religious intolerance, the
Judaic element in the Christian ethos, and by a continuous
interchange of these terms giddy the reasoning faculty of the
reader—and you will get the betrayal of Christianity into
Christian anti-Semitism by the "Judaic element" in the Christian ethos.[73]

<h2 style="text-align:center">3.</h2>

Notwithstanding his sophistry, one cannot help having some
sympathy with Mr. Toynbee. Having extolled the towering
superiority of the essentially new Christian departure as compared with Judaism, he is badly let down by the Christian
performance in history in general, and not only in the specific
case of anti-Semitism. He cannot overlook the intolerance and
the violence with which the religion of gentleness and love
treated other religions and philosophies of life or Christian
deviations from orthodoxy and the officially approved religious
dogma or belief. According to Mr. Toynbee the evidence of
history is so condemning that he does not hesitate to declare:
"There has been no religion in which this fanaticism—this
persecution of all heterodox opinions without regard for the
consequences and without shrinking from any crime—has
been, and remained, so dominant as it has been in Christianity
in all its manifestations."[74] This, of course, requires an explanation, and Mr. Toynbee finds it in the unpleasantly close association between Judaism and Christianity. For reasons of ex-
igency, it appears, Christianity, after having taken "a decisive
new departure from Judaism," readmitted "the incongruous
Israelitish concept and service of 'the Jealous God' Yahweh."[75]

It is thence that intolerance and religious fanaticism entered the body of Christendom.

Once again the Toynbean method of ignoring logical inconsistencies and contradictions is apparent. One might wonder what could be meant by the *readmission* of the incongruous Israelitish service of the Jealous God. According to his theological version of Judaism, the pre-exilic prophets of Israel and Judah had overcome the earlier tribal concepts and found the way of gentleness and Transfiguration. Christianity had no contact with "the Israelitish Jealous God," in the Toynbean sense of the term. That concept was abrogated by Judaism about eight or nine centuries before Christianity came into being, and about twelve centuries before its "readmission" into Christianity—with the beginning of Christian intolerance—is supposed to have occurred. Mr. Toynbee's psychological version of Judaism alone brings the intolerant and jealous god right to the doorstep of Christianity. On that basis, however, although there is proximity in time there is hardly any association in spirit. As we have heard, Jewry never really got beyond the concept of the tribal deity, "widened" by psychological escapism. It was only the Christian Church, on the one hand, and Rabbi Johanan ben Zakkai, on the other—but also in the "Christian" manner—which by way of Transfiguration discovered the One True God. Seen in this light, Christianity was regarded as a radically new departure from the Judaism of the Jealous God, inheriting from it nothing more than the bankruptcy of Futurism. Christianity was no kindred religion of that Judaism, and Judaism was no component part of it.

The dilemma does not disturb Mr. Toynbee; he mixes his frames of reference without a qualm. The theological version of Judaism proved that the Jewish religious genius took refuge in Christianity; the psychological version proved that the Israelitish tribal deity was fanatically intolerant. It is true that the Jewish religious genius, absorbed by Christianity, is the genius of the ethos of gentleness, and that the intolerant tribal deity has no connection whatever with Christianity; nevertheless, if we pretend that the words "Jewish," "Judaism," and "Israelitish" are always used with the same meaning and that

31

the two versions of "Judaic" development are not what they really are—namely, a contradiction—we do get the "conclusion" that the world-wide Christian intolerance that mars Western history is due to the *readmission* of the "Israelitish concept and service of the Jealous God."

We may now understand why Mr. Toynbee, having built up such a powerful case for the separation of Christianity from Judaism, nevertheless retains the association between them that derives from his earlier, theological interpretation of Judaism. In truth, Christianity is a "decisive new departure" in all essential teachings and dogmas. But it is useful not to renounce the traditionally assumed contact with Judaism; that contact enables one to exculpate the religion of love for its crimes of fanaticism and intolerance by blaming them on the readmission of barbarous Judaic concepts. The ambiguities of style, the literary trickery, and the confusion of the frames of reference give us still another version of Judaism, under which it may be considered Christianity's "original sin." There seems to be no escape from the power of that original sin. It is responsible not only for Christian fanaticism, but even for the intolerance of the "neo-pagan" Western secular enlightenment. This is because "a post-Christian Western rationalism . . . inherited from Christianity a Judaic fanaticism and intolerance in its feelings and its conduct towards its adversaries."[76] Thus Christian religious and post-Christian secular fanaticism and persecutions both originate from the Judaic element introduced into the West by Christianity. Thus, Mr. Toynbee provides the "scholarly" backing for what the Nazis knew instinctively, namely, that "the Jews are our misfortune." If only Christianity had been more careful with whom it kept company in its early youth!

II. THE JUDAISM OF THE JEWS

1. THE TRIBAL DEITY AND "DEUTERO-ISAIAH"

THUS FAR we have analyzed the theories of Mr. Toynbee, remaining on his own ground and showing what his ideas contain and what use he makes of them. We shall now attempt to outline a Jewish approach to the issues that have been discussed.

Fortunately, there is no need to deal at length with Mr. Toynbee's psychological version of the development of Judaism from the tribal-religion stage. Whatever the theological and historical truth about such a development, it is preposterous and irresponsible to place it in the post-exilic period from 525 B.C.E. to 70 C.E., as Mr. Toynbee does. Anyone who does so cannot expect to be treated seriously as a scholar. We shall therefore limit ourselves to Mr. Toynbee's fantastic falsification of the message of "Deutero-Isaiah." On the basis of the single phrase, "Thus saith the Lord to His anointed, to Cyrus,"[1] he imputes to the prophet the mundane megalomaniac attempt to cajole Cyrus into handing over his empire to a puny and broken Jewry. If only Mr. Toynbee had taken notice of the contents of the chapter from which he quotes the phrase to prove his point! In the same chapter, one may also find such pronouncements as these about God, salvation, mankind, and Israel:

For thus saith the Lord that created the heavens,
He is God;
That formed the earth and made it,
He established it,
He created it not a waste, He formed it to be inhabited:
I am the Lord, and there is none else.

. . . .

And there is no God else beside Me;
A just God and a *Saviour;*

33

There is none beside Me.
Look unto Me, and *be ye saved,*
All the ends of the earth;
For I am God, and there is none else.
By Myself have I sworn,
The word is gone forth from My mouth in righteousness.

. . . .

That unto Me every knee shall bow,
Every tongue shall swear.
Only in the Lord, shall one say of Me,
Is victory and strength;
Even to Him shall men come in confusion,
All they that were incensed against Him.
In the Lord shall all the seed of Israel
Be justified, and shall glory.

In order to appreciate the vileness of the Toynbean distortion of "Deutero-Isaiah," one must read, against the background of these quotations from only one chapter of the prophet, Mr. Toynbee's interpretation of the introductory verses in the same chapter. According to him that is what the prophet hoped for:

The mundane kingdom which is included in "Deutero-Isaiah's" Kingdom of God is imagined as an Achaemenian Empire in which Cyrus has taken Zion instead of Susa for his capital and the Jews instead of the Persians for his ruling race, because the God of Israel has revealed to him that it is he (*and, by implication, not Ahuramazda*[2]) who has enabled Cyrus to conquer the World. In this day-dream "Deutero-Isaiah" is exposing himself with a vengeance, to the censure of our imaginary psycho-analyst.[3] He is conscripting Yahweh to inspire Cyrus to turn the feats of Persian arms to the benefit of the Jews in order that the latter may be compensated for their inability to preserve the independence of their own petty principality of Judah by being invested with the lordship of a universal state! Jewry's thirst to gain a new mundane kingdom was so deep that the Jewish prophet was prepared to recognize the Gentile as "the Lord's Anointed" if that would secure the fulfilment of these Jewish hopes.[4]

As if this were not clear enough, Mr. Toynbee paraphrases the opening words of the same chapter in the following manner:

> Thus saith the Lord to his Anointed, to Cyrus (or Zerubbabel or Simon Maccabaeus or Simon bar Kokaba or whatever may be the name of the hero of the hour), whose right hand I have holden to subdue nations before him . . .[5]

The truth of course is—and it is certainly not hidden from Mr. Toynbee—that, as we have seen, in this chapter of the Book of Isaiah the basic Jewish concepts of a universal ethical monotheism find clear expression. There is the Lord God, creator and sustainer of the Universe, whose word is righteousness and who alone is savior of all mankind, in whom alone Israel seeks its justification.[6] Cyrus is an instrument in the hand of God, just as the Assyrian conqueror was so designated by Isaiah.[7] It is the well-known concept of the prophets that God intervenes in the history of the nations by raising and using world-conquerors to do His bidding in the world at large. What is expected of Cyrus is not Toynbee's idiotic idea of surrendering world dominion to the Jews, but an act of charity toward captive Judah, as it is stated unequivocally in the context: "He shall build My city, and he shall let Mine exiles go free, not for price nor reward. . . ." It is the age-old plea of "Let my people go." The conquest of the nations and the spoliation of their treasures are the due of the world-conqueror Cyrus, as it was that of Nebuchadnezzar. As for the Jews, they seek their "justification and glory" in the Lord, who alone is "a just God and a Saviour and besides whom there is none."

Nothing more clearly shows Mr. Toynbee's intellectual dishonesty than his misrepresentation of "Deutero-Isaiah," the prophet who created the immortal figure of "the Suffering Servant of the Lord."[8] In Christian belief and theology "Deutero-Isaiah" is the cornerstone of the prophetic testimony for the mission of Jesus. It is from the eternally living words of this Jewish prophet that Mr. Toynbee himself quotes in order to describe most adequately his own idea of the savior.[9] In a sense, it would be even true to say that the prophet's "Suffering Servant" is the key to the understanding of Mr. Toynbee's *Study*. Nevertheless, when our author tries to determine the place of the same "Deutero-Isaiah" in Judaism and Jewish history, he calls him "a day-dreamer" who exposed himself "with a vengeance to the censure" of a psychoanalyst. One cannot help wondering what becomes of the christological testimony and Mr. Toynbee's own savior, if a few sessions with a psychoanalyst might have been enough to cure "Deutero-Isaiah" of his "escapism." Is "Deutero-Isaiah" a day-dreaming, anxiety-ridden neurotic only when he testifies against Mr. Toynbee's pet theories? Does he become a divinely inspired witness and prophet only when he appears to fit into the Toynbean universe?

2. The Meaning of the Maccabean Struggle and of the Zealot Rebellions against Rome

Since Mr. Toynbee's psychological version of Judaic development has no basis either in theology or in history, we shall discuss his interpretations of the Maccabean and Zealot attitudes as described by him on the basis of the premises of his theological version of Judaism.

As already stated, the Maccabees were no creators in the realm of Judaism. Whether their policies were right or wrong, there never existed a "Maccabean Judaism" or a Maccabean "Church Militant." What Mr. Toynbee is unable to understand is that Judaism has been embodied not in a church but in a people. In the history of a people, constituted by a religion, the mundane and religious elements cannot be neatly separated from each other. In the Maccabean wars, political freedom was the precondition of religious freedom. In view of the oppressive legislation of Antiochus Epiphanes, which forbade the practice of Judaism under penalty of death, Jews—if they wanted to remain Jews—had to be free. The military and political struggle subserved the religious purpose. That is the only conclusion one may draw from the records available. The Maccabees fought for liberty, imbued by the conviction, as Judah Maccabee put it, that as liberty "is a thing of itself agreeable to all men, so it proves to be to us much more desirable, by its affording us the liberty of worshipping God."[10]

Although with the Maccabees the religious motivation was more pronounced, probably with the Zealots under the Roman Empire the goal of national liberty was more in the foreground. But even with them it is hardly possible to separate the mundane plane of life from the religious. Describing the philosophy of the various sects among the Jews, Josephus says of the Zealots: "These men agree in all other things with the Pharisaic notions; but they have an inviolable attachment to liberty, and say, that God is to be their only Ruler and Lord."[11] The thought that a servant of God calls no man his lord is deeply religious, and it is unlikely that either the Maccabees or the Zealots ever associated the idea of liberty with a "mundane" meaning, as Toynbee wants it.

The Maccabean and Zealot wars had one important feature in common: they were provoked by insults to the basic religious convictions of Jewry and inspired by the threat to their spiritual survival. The Seleucid era in Judea began after the battle of Gaza. As early as 312 B.C.E. Jewry became the subject people of the Hellenized kingdom of Syria, but they never rebelled as long as there was no interference with their religious and spiritual life. About 150 years after the loss of political freedom to the Seleucids, the Maccabean revolt started when— by the order of Antiochus Epiphanes—an "abomination of desolation" was set up in the Temple of Jerusalem and the practice of Judaism was forbidden in all the land. The situation was rather similar at the time of the last Jewish rebellions against the yoke of the Roman Empire about three centuries later. The revolt of Bar Kokba broke out when Hadrian on the ruins of Jerusalem established his own city of Aelia Capitolina and on the place of the Temple of the One True God erected a temple of Jupiter.[12]

Even though the threat to Judaism was not as obvious at the

moment of the actual beginning of the Zealot war with Rome, it was deeply embedded in the real causes of that insurrection too. The same generation of Jews that was driven, by the barbarity of the brigand procurators of the type of Antonius Felix and Gessius Florus,[13] to the revolt of despair, had still fresh in its memory two significant incidents that very nearly anticipated the Zealot war by twenty-five or thirty-five years. They still recalled the calculated insult to their religious faith by Pontius Pilate, who—breaking with established custom—displayed in Jerusalem the Roman military standards bearing the effigies of Caesar, which he removed only as the result of the determined resistance of the entire people. When, several years after Pilate's procuratorship, the emperor Caligula insisted that his statue be set up in the Temple of Jerusalem and granted divine honors, the challenge to the survival of Judaism was no less serious than at the time of Antiochus Epiphanes. Only the death of Caligula (41 c.e.) averted, temporarily, the catastrophe that finally culminated in 66-69 c.e.

Mr. Toynbee makes light of these manifestations of the faith-inspired resistance of Jewry during the Maccabean and Zealot wars. He does not mention them when he builds his theory of the "transformation" of Judaism in a political instrument in a mundane struggle. He refers to them under the incongruous heading, "The Utility of a Monetary Currency as a Medium for Governmental Propaganda." Having mentioned the indignation of the Jews at the placing of the statue of the Olympian Zeus in the Holy of Holies of the Temple of Jerusalem, which did not allow them "to rest until they had thrown off every vestige of Seleucid rule"; and having also noted the vehement reaction to Pontius Pilate's smuggling of the Roman military standards into Jerusalem under the cover of darkness, Toynbee continues: "Yet in their holy land the Jews had schooled themselves meekly, not only to seeing, but to handling, using, earning, hoarding, and by all these compromising actions progressively countenancing, the abominable image on Caesar's coinage, and had thereby anticipated in action the observation of their future Roman chastiser Vespasian that sordid money does not smell." In order to catch a good glimpse of the Toynbean mentality, one should read this passage from the *Study*[14] together with what a Prussian historian has to say on the same subject. In an essay on the "Ghetto and Jews of Rome," Ferdinand Gregorovius makes the following observation:

Caligula had special grounds for his bitterness against the Jews. He had conceived the idea of having a colossal statue of himself in the character of a god set up in the Holy of Holies of the Temple at Jerusalem, for he had learned that the Jewish people alone among the nations of the earth had refused to grant him divine honors. He issued orders to Petronius, the governor of Phoenicia, to have the statue set up. Thereupon, as Josephus and Philo relate, all Judea, men, women, children, and the aged, betook themselves to Phoenicia. They covered the country like a cloud, and so loud was their lament that even when it ceased its echoes reverberated through the air. They threw themselves upon their knees before Petronius and adjured him to slay them all, weaponless as they were: they would never suffer the sanctuary of God to be desecrated. The scene represents one of the most magnificent tragedies a people has ever experienced, and the moral resistance they offered to Caligula is one of the most admirable episodes in the history of the Jewish people, shedding more glory upon them than the greatest achievements of David and Solomon.[15]

This episode, which so deeply impressed a Petronius that he implored Caligula to rescind his order and in which the Prussian historian admires the magnificent tragedy of moral resistance, moves Mr. Toynbee only to a scurrilous anti-Semitic joke. Our main concern is, however, with his falsification of history in this connection. He asserts that the reason for the toleration of Judaism as compared with the persecution of Christianity under Nero and his successors was that the Christians refused "to accept the Government's claim that it was entitled to compel its subjects to act against their consciences." Similarly, he maintains that the subjects and peoples of the Hellenic universal state, out of a sense of gratitude for peace and unity, "without much heart searchings" acquiesced in the deification of the Caesars; it was only with the advent of Christianity that the concept was challenged.[16] The truth is, as we have seen, that it was the Jewish people of the Seleucid and Roman empires who alone among all the nations refused to accept any dictation to their conscience and resisted any suggestion of Caesaro-worship. This was the common religious inspiration of the Maccabean and Zealot periods in Jewish history, whether the fight against the oppressor of their conscience was conducted with or without weapons. The primitive Christians were following the Jewish example.[17]

Since, contrary to all proof, Mr. Toynbee tenaciously clings to his "mundane" version of the Maccabean wars, he does not understand the nature of the Maccabean accomplishment. It is true that if the Maccabees had been concerned with the restoration of a "mundane" national kingdom, their success would have been short-lived and effaced by the final defeat at the hands of the Romans. As it was, the Maccabean victories brought about the defeat of Antiochus Epiphanes and, through it, the defeat of the Hellenic temptation for the Jewish soul. The Maccabees conquered Jewry for Judaism and, without them, it is doubtful whether Christianity would even have had a chance to be born. Because the Maccabean victory was essentially accomplished within the Jewish soul, the material conquest of Zealot Jewry by Rome on the battlefield could not undo the Maccabean achievement. Mr. Toynbee is perfectly right in his condemnation of the forcible conversion of some Gentiles by one or two of the Hasmonean princes. It might have helped him to understand the significance of that episode for Jewry and Judaism, had he followed the method of Jewish historians and distinguished the Maccabean period from the Hasmonean. The Maccabees were *the people* under the leadership of a family that emerged from the midst of the people; the Hasmoneans were a dynasty that became more and more estranged from the people and their recognized leaders, the Pharisees. Imitating the petty potentates around them, they degenerated at times into a tyranny. For instance, Alexander Jannai—the only Hasmonean whom Mr. Toynbee mentions by name—was probably more ruthless in his long civil wars, fought with foreign mercenaries against his own people, than in his foreign wars against neighboring Gentile nations. The religious conversions undertaken by some Hasmoneans were dictated by their personal dynastic policies; they occurred in two dangerous frontier districts for the purpose of military safety. To see in these Hasmonean princes representatives of Judaism, and in their policies the manifestation of Jewish religious intolerance, is about as justified as, for example, to see Henry VIII as a paragon of Christianity, and his marital affairs as a change in the Christian ethos.[18] In footnotes and annexes Mr. Toynbee occasionally allows his readers a fleeting glance at the truth, which he distorts and falsifies in his main text; and so he grants the Pharisees the credit "that they did not let themselves drift with the tide of popular feeling, but parted company with the Maccabees just when, and just because, the Maccabees put their treasure in the establishment of an earthly kingdom."[19] This is the closest Mr. Toynbee ever gets to the acknowledgment of the truth. The Pharisees did part company with some of the Hasmonean princes, and particularly with Alexander Jannai, for the reasons indicated; they did not part company with the Maccabees. When the Pharisees broke with the Hasmonean dynasty, with them went the people. This, however, is again another aspect of history to which a man whose only sources on Judaism are the New Testament and Eduard Meyer dare not open his eyes.

3. The Ethos of Judaism in the Maccabean and Zealot Periods

During his lengthy and repetitive discussion of the Maccabees and the Zealots, Mr. Toynbee pretends that these were the leaders and teachers in Judaism and that what they represented was the Judaic ethos. If they fought in wars, then war is consecrated by Jewish tradition[20]; if Hasmonean princes converted some Gentiles by force, then "a fanatical religious intolerance" is the very essence of Judaism. Nothing is more characteristic of this intellectual perversion than Mr. Toynbee's cherished

41

contrast between the gentleness of Jesus and the militancy of a
Theudas or a Judas of Galilee. He elaborates on it, he comes
back to it again and again; it typifies for him the two ways in
history, exemplified by Christian gentleness and Judaic violence.[21] But who were Theudas and Judas of Galilee? What
was their place in Judaism and its history? Like hundreds of
others of their generation, they were patriots, who in the par-
lance of all oppressors and their Herodian underlings against
whom patriots ever revolted in history, were referred to as
brigands. Theudas and Judas owe their notoriety mainly to the
fact that they are mentioned in the New Testament. But what
a comparison for an historian to make—between Jesus and the
Jewish Robin Hood or Davy Crockett! Here gentle Christianity
—there violent Judaism!

The recognized teachers and interpreters of Judaism, who in
most cases were also the leaders of Jewry, their teachings, their
philosophy, their religious and ethical tenets, their manner of
life and death—all are completely ignored by Mr. Toynbee.
The friendliest thing one may say about him is that he is an
ignoramus. If he had obtained a Jewish prayer book and
turned to the section which contains a part of the Mishnah
which is normally translated as "Ethics of the Fathers," he
would have found the names of the outstanding leader and
teacher of each generation of Jewry, beginning with the Seleucid era and concluding with the time of the Hadrian persecutions, which followed the Bar Kokba debacle. The chain of
tradition outlined in the first chapter covers the entire period
which is interpreted by Mr. Toynbee. The few dicta handed
down there in the names of the leading teachers of Israel might
have helped our author to gain some slight inkling of the
spirit of Judaism in the Maccabean and Zealot phases of Jewish
history.

At the opening of the Seleucid era he would have come across
the adage by Simon the Just, the High Priest, that the world
was based on three things: the Torah, religious worship, and
the practice of loving-kindness. At the end of the entire era
under survey stands the figure of Rabban Simon ben Gamliel,
the head of the Sanhedrin, who died a martyr's death during

the Hadrianic persecutions. One of his maxims, a variation on the theme of Simon the Just, stated that the world was preserved by three things: by truth, by justice, and by peace. "As it is said: execute the judgment of truth and peace in your gates."[22] Concerning the mundane expectations of Jewry, Mr. Toynbee might have pondered over the teaching of Antigonos of Socho, a disciple of Simon the Just, who said of the service of God: "Be not like servants who minister to their master upon the condition of receiving a reward; but like servants who minister to their master without the condition of receiving a reward."[23] Concerning the authentic Judaic attitude toward Herod and Herodianism, Mr. Toynbee might have consulted the policy statement of Shemayah, one of the leaders of the Pharisees, the teacher of Hillel, the man who with dignity and courage stood up to the Hasmonean king Hyrcanus and the young but already powerful Herod, when the latter was accused in the Sanhedrin of murder. It is the same Shemayah who advised the people of Jerusalem to admit Herod peacefully to the capital, when Herod together with Sosius besieged Jerusalem, but under whose guidance the Pharisees refused to take the oath of loyalty to Herod, the King by the grace of Rome.[24] The Judaic attitude toward the times and their problems was expressed by Shemayah and preservèd in the first chapter of the "Ethics of the Fathers": "Love work, hate lordship, and seek no intimacy with the mundane authority." Concerning the Jewish ethos of militancy, Hillel, the great disciple of the great master, might have provided Mr. Toynbee with some useful information. His maxim was: "Be of the disciples of Aaron, loving peace and pursuing peace, loving thy fellow-creatures, and drawing them near to the Torah."

While these few maxims do throw some light on the subject which Mr. Toynbee discusses with such impressive pretense of authority, they are like a drop in the ocean compared with the full extent of the Judaic teaching of the Maccabean and Zealot periods. Mr. Toynbee, however, is not a perfect ignoramus on the subject of the Judaism of those days. His claim to perfection is marred by one quotation from the sayings of Rabbi Johanan ben Zakkai. After the destruction of the Temple, Rabbi

Johanan comforted his disciple, Rabbi Joshua, that the practice of loving-kindness was equal to the Temple service in propitiating for the sins of Israel. But, as often, a little knowledge is more dangerous than none. Having quoted the above saying from a second-hand source, Mr. Toynbee proceeds to base on it another one of the theories of his fertile imagination: "In act and word Johanan ben Zakkai was proclaiming his *conversion* from the way of Violence to the way of Gentleness; and through this conversion he became *the founder of a new Jewry* . . ."[25] Nothing could be further from the truth. Mr. Toynbee's only justification for mentioning the "conversion" of Rabbi Johanan ben Zakkai is his own misrepresentation of Judaism as "a way of Violence." Had our author taken even one glance at the original source from which his informants quote, he might have understood that the Rabbi was the head of the peace party in besieged Jerusalem.[26] The suggestion that Rabbi Johanan was "the founder of a new Jewry" is an utterly unjustified invention. He lived and taught in the spirit of his great master Hillel, with whom his personal relationship was one of touching mutual love and respect. On his sick bed the old, perhaps dying, Hillel called Rabbi Johanan, who was the youngest among his disciples, "Father of Wisdom and Father of his Generation."[27] And, when the disciple was later recognized by all as the "Father of the Generation," he extolled the greatness of his masters by declaring, with self-effacing modesty, that all his wisdom he received from his masters; yet it compared to what they possessed as the amount of water that a fly, which dips into the sea and flies away again, takes away from the ocean.[28] The very quotation Mr. Toynbee takes from the teachings of Rabbi Johanan ben Zakkai proves the continuity of the Judaic ethos throughout generations; for the Rabbi used for the "bestowal of kindness"—or the practice of loving-kindness—the same Hebrew expression that had been used, four centuries earlier, by Simon the Just, when he said that it constituted one of the foundations of the world.[29]

While there may be some excuse for ignorance, there is none for intellectual dishonesty. When Mr. Toynbee discusses the reactions of Jewry to the impact of the Roman Empire, he

JUDAISM—FOSSIL OR FERMENT?

acknowledges only "Herodianism" and "Zealotism."[30] Characteristically, however, he does mention the existence of a strong peace party in Jerusalem when one would least expect it—in the chapter on "The Psychological Consequences of Atomic Warfare!" When he there discusses the possibilities of "heroism which is beyond Reason because it is above it," he cannot suppress the example of Jewry in the years of their wars against the Roman Empire. In order to impress upon his readers the satanic addiction of Jewry to violence, Mr. Toynbee has underscored the obvious hopelessness of the Zealot reaction to Rome. But here, surely, was a fine example of "heroism which is beyond Reason because it is above it"; and a Jewish reader prepares himself to get—for a change—a few words of praise for his distant ancestors. He is mistaken again. For Mr. Toynbee hastens now to unearth the peace party and says: "It is, however, significant that in Jerusalem . . . a *majority* of the besieged would have countenanced overtures for forestalling extermination by surrender, if they had not been *terrorized by a minority of fanatics* into participating in these Zealots' suicidal heroism."[31] The Zealots in their violence are identical with Jewry; in their heroism they are only "a minority of fanatics." As a matter of principle, Mr. Toynbee always acknowledges the truth—when to ignore it might be more flattering to Judaism and Jewry than to recognize it. He does not recognize the philosophy of the peace party as one of the Jewish attitudes at the time of the crisis. Yet, it is within the peace party that Mr. Toynbee would have found the teachers of Jewry and interpreters of Judaism, the majority of the Pharisees together with the majority of the besieged.

4. ETHOS AND MILITANCY

Nothing could be less justified than the Toynbean contrast between the gentle Christian response and the violent "Judaic" one. Not only does he ignore the life and teachings of the recognized interpreters of Judaism, and the implementation of their ethos in the policies of a strong peace party, but he covers up the important point that the Christian response to

45

the challenge of the times, the response of Jesus and his disciples, as well as that of the Christian apostle Paul, was in reality part of the Jewish response. This was not only because the founders and the apostles of Christianity were themselves Jews, but mainly because their ethos of gentleness was deeply embedded in the prophetic and Pharisaic tradition of the Jewry whose children they were too. It was the Jewish prophet Isaiah through whom the message of God was conveyed to Israel: "In sitting still and rest shall ye be saved, in quietness and in confidence shall be your strength. . . ."[32] To Zerubbabel, whose activity—in the Toynbean distortion—is to create the nucleus of the mundane world empire of the Messiah, the charge is: "This is the word of the Lord unto Zerubbabel, saying: 'Not by might, nor by power, but by My spirit, saith the Lord of hosts.'"[33]

The fact that gentleness is not surrender, but rather the answer to a challenge on the spiritual plane, is fully realized by Mr. Toynbee. The Spirit of the Lord is itself the most powerful weapon. Thus he tells us, for example, that Paul "seizes upon all the noble and glorious connotations of War" in order to convey, "in a chain of military metaphors, the more ethereal glory and nobility of the Christian life." Mr. Toynbee also maintains that "this use of military metaphor in the Epistles of Saint Paul is the *first step*—and a long one—towards a transfiguration of the word 'War' from a physical to a spiritual meaning."[34] The truth is that, far from taking the "first step," the Christian apostle only reflects the unsurpassed pronouncements of the Jewish prophets. Toynbee's quotation is from the Second Epistle to the Corinthians:

> Though we walk in the flesh, we do not war after the flesh (for the weapons of our warfare are not carnal, but mighty through God to the pulling down of strongholds): casting down imaginations, and every high thing that exalteth itself against the knowledge of God, and bringing into captivity every thought to the obedience of Christ.

To a Jewish ear the passage sounds like good orthodox Jewish teaching. Without the one reference to "obedience of Christ"

—which may easily be replaced by "obedience of God"—it might pass for a Pharisaic comment on such verses from the prophets as these:

Behold, I have put My *words* in thy mouth;
See, I have this day set thee over the nations and over the
  kingdoms,
To root out and to pull down,
And to destroy and to overthrow;
To build, and to plant.[35]

Since the words are addressed to the one solitary man, Jeremiah, who is set up over nations and kingdoms, it is obvious that his weapons are but the words of God in his mouth—a fact so tragically confirmed by the prophet's consequent life of suffering and sorrow.

But the mightiest step "towards a transfiguration of the word 'War' from a physical to a spiritual meaning" had been taken eight centuries before Paul, by Isaiah, who in his immortal Messianic vision said of the shoot that shall come forth "out of the stock of Jesse":

And the spirit of the Lord shall rest upon him,
The spirit of wisdom and understanding,

. . . .

And he shall smite the land with the *rod of his mouth,*
And with the *breath of his lips* shall he slay the wicked.
And *righteousness* shall be the *girdle of his loins,*
And *faithfulness* the *girdle of his reins.*

The Judaic transfiguration of war into conquering spiritual potency on earth is completed by the vision of universal reconciliation and eternal peace, when the Jewish prophet concludes:

And the wolf shall dwell with the lamb,
And the leopard shall lie down with the kid;
And the calf and the young kids and the fatling together;
And a little child shall lead them.

. . . .

They shall not hurt nor destroy
In all my holy mountain;

47

For the earth shall be full of the knowledge of the Lord,
As the waters cover the sea.[36]

Beyond this, no further steps are needed toward the "transfiguration of the word 'war' "—nor have they ever been taken
by anyone.

As we saw, the Judaic ethos of gentleness continued to be
taught—without a break in the chain of tradition—by the
great Pharisaic teachers from Simon the Just to Rabbi Johanan
ben Zakkai.[37] Even the *law of Karma* to which the "Saviour
with the Sword" is subject, and which Toynbee finds expressed
in the basic teaching of Jesus that "All they that take the sword
shall perish with the sword,"[38] is of Pharisaic origin. It was
formulated in the generation before Jesus by Hillel, who—on
seeing "a skull floating on the surface of the water—said to it:
'Because thou drownedst others, they have drowned thee, and
at the last they that drowned thee shall themselves be
drowned.' "[39]

Our purpose, however, is not to lay claim to the Jewish or-
igins of the Christian ethos, but—as already indicated—to
establish the fact that the "Christian" response to the crisis of
the times during the Roman procuratorship and immediately
after the fall of Jerusalem has to be understood as one aspect
of the Jewish answer to the challenge. It could not have been
the Christian answer, since Christianity had not been in existence prior to it. It was the response of Jews, involved in the
struggle of their Jewish people and seeking an answer to the
Jewish problems of their generation in the spirit of Jewish
tradition, that gave birth to Christianity. The "Christian" response was as much part of the Jewish reaction as was "Zealotism," and certainly much more so than "Herodianism." The
three forms of Jewish reaction to the intrusion of the Hellenic
universal state upon Jewry were Zealotism, Pharisaism, and
Christianity. The Zealots, as we saw, were not without religious
zeal; with them religious and political freedom coalesced. They
attempted to build "the Kingdom" with the sword. The Pharisees, men without power of office and without a sword, were
the leaders of the people "by the breath of their lips." They

wanted peace on the terms of the policy of Shemaya, by with-drawing from political life. The "Christians" among the Jews, by overemphasizing the Judaic ethos of gentleness, found their answer in turning away not only from political activism but from "this World" altogether. If Judaism and Jewry of the time are to be blamed for Zealotism, then Judaism and Jewry ought to be credited with Christianity.

For a Jew, this is not a matter of pride, but one of historic relevance. If a historian wishes to exemplify the Christian re-sponse of a society to a crisis, he must not point to the case of Jewry in the process of producing Christianity. He should offer as an illustration the behavior of an *already* Christian society, the reaction of a Christian people or civilization to a challenge similar to the one with which Jewry was faced at the time of Jesus. Mr. Toynbee does seem to make such an attempt when he draws a comparison between the primitive Christians and the Jewish people. Says our author: "In striking contrast to the series of Jewish insurrections... the Christians never once rose in armed revolt against their Roman persecutors during the approximately equal period of time that elapsed between the beginning of Jesus' mission and the conclusion of peace and alliance."[40] But must one remind an eminent historian like Mr. Toynbee that one does not compare "equal periods of time" with each other? He knows well enough that comparisons be-tween societies and civilization are permissible only on the basis of correlative phases of their development. It is a tech-nique that he himself employs with great fervor throughout his entire *Study;* it forms the basis of all his "law-making" in history.

The Jewish insurrections were undertaken by a people, living in their own native land and assaulted by a ruthless invader. The primitive Christians were not a people but members of a religious sect; they were not living in one society concentrated on its native soil, but scattered abroad and lodged in handfuls in the midst of an overwhelming majority of non-Christians.[41] One should compare Jewry's behavior at the time of these in-surrections with that of a Christian society attacked on its own soil by an aggressor. Is there in all history a single example of

49

a Christian people or civilization that, when attacked in its homeland, remembered the Christian ethos of gentleness and put away the sword because "All they that take the sword shall perish with the sword?" The answer is obvious. It also emerges clearly from what Mr. Toynbee himself has to say on the subject. Immediately after the "conclusion of peace and alliance" with the Roman Empire, the "Christians abandoned the policy of toleration with alacrity as soon as they became conscious that in material strength, they had acquired a decisive superiority. . . ."[42] On the encounter of the modern West with the Jews, the Eastern Orthodox Christians, and the Muslims, Mr. Toynbee has the following to say: "These neighbours of the West remembered her, since the time of the Crusades, as a military aggressive society whose aggressiveness had been aggravated by a fanatical zeal to impose on all mankind her local Western version of Christianity."[43] It is equally clear that the records of the modern "parochial" states and nations of Western Christendom are no less devastating. It would therefore seem that in all history the only society that did give, at least through one of its factions, a "Christian response" to the challenge of a serious crisis has been the Jewish people in its struggle with the Romano-Hellenic empire.[44]

Mr. Toynbee battles bravely to explain the failure of Western Christendom to abide by the gentle ethos of Christianity. When, for a while, he loses sight of Judaism and Jewry, he is an honest man. And so he builds up a rationalist's accusation against the four living Higher Religions, among which—of course—Judaism does not figure. The rationalist case is that we can extol religion at the cost of secular civilization only by resorting to a trick, which "is, after all, a simple one. You have merely to ascribe to a church the virtues preached in the scriptures attributed to the church's founder and your church inevitably takes the highest place on the ladder." The trick, however, is easy to unmask. All one has to do is to direct one's attention from "the alleged ideals of the church's founder to the current practice of the church. . . . Look around you. . . . Behold Christianity, the Mahayana, Islam, and Hinduism not as they claim to be but as they are. . . ."[45] A Jewish reader is amused by such an honest exchange of ideas between the author and an imagined rationalist, because the rationalist not only defends the claim of civilization as compared with religion but exactly describes the method used by Mr. Toynbee in order to create the "antithesis" between Christian gentleness and Jewish violence. Christianity is what Jesus teaches; Judaism, what some Jews (not even the most representative among them) do.

Mr. Toynbee's answer to the rationalist accusation is not to deny that there is a tragic gulf between ideal and performance in the Higher Religions, but to assert that the rationalist should remain true to his own premises and measure the past and the future of the churches by the "time-scale established by a Modern Western Physical Science." On that time-scale, compared to the age of the earth and the physical universe, "a period of nineteen or twenty centuries, so far from being 'a long time,' was no more than the twinkling of an eye. . . ."[46] So, have patience; even if religion has failed thus far, what do a mere nineteen centuries amount to, when man looks forward to a future that is to be counted in millions of years! Be that as it may, one is puzzled by the fact that a historian who has nothing more to say in defense of Christianity should have the impudence to condemn Judaism, to speak of its "ethos of violence," on the basis of the actions of a minority group in Jewry at one period in its history.

Our purpose in dwelling on all this is not to say to Mr. Toynbee: "And why beholdest thou the mote that is in thy brother's eye, but considerest not the beam that is in thine own eye?" The subject which he grandiloquently calls "The Challenge of Militancy on Earth"[47] when he labors to explain the "spiritual regression" of the Papacy and Christianity, but which he ignores completely in his discussion of the Maccabees and Zealots, provides a useful illustration for a better understanding of the Jewish position. The final conclusion of Mr. Toynbee seems to be that, on account of "Original Sin, spiritual regression, as witnessed in the history of Christendom, is inescapable; the gulf between the ideal and the performance remains unbridgeable and, "so long as Original Sin continued to be an element in terrestrial Human Nature, there would always be work in This World for Caesar to do. . . ."[48] Mr. Toynbee does not believe in progress in the usual sense of the word. Human nature has not changed much in the past, nor is there, as long as Original Sin remains, reason to expect any significant change in the future. The "Christian hope of a spiritually new species of personality, of which the first-fruits had already been manifested in Christ and in the Saints, might never receive fulfilment in a regeneration of Mankind in the mass. . . ."[49]

A non-Christian, who does not accept the dogma of Original Sin, will have to come to fundamentally different conclusions about the gulf between the ideals and the performance of the West; nor need he accept the defeatist dictum concerning the improbability of "a regeneration of Mankind in the mass." It may just be that in order to regenerate the human race methods are needed which are different from those that have so conspicuously failed in the past. It may well be that the Pharisaic teachers and leaders of Jewry saw further than is generally assumed. As we have already had occasion to remark, Judaism was never embodied in a church but always in a people. We shall yet see what significance is to be attached to such a statement. In the meantime suffice it to say that the Pharisees, being responsible not for the doctrines of a church but for the Judaic life of a people, fully appreciated the fact that ideals, including that of gentleness, were not lacking in Jewry, as they are hardly ever lacking in any society. The thing that mattered for them was not to escape from "this World" but *in* it to implement the Word of God.

III. THE JUDAISM OF THE JEWS
(continued)

1. GOD AS POWER AND GOD AS LOVE

1.

ONE OF THE purposes of Mr. Toynbee's psychological version
of Judaism is to provide Jewish intolerance with a foundation
in Judaism itself. How could Jewry not be intolerant if its God
was never able to shake off completely its tribal past? The
Israelitish God is jealous and He manifests Himself in His
might. And so we get another antithesis: here the Israelitish
dispensation that God is Power, there the Christian revelation
that God is Love. There is, of course, nothing very original
about this. It is a mere rumination of the old commonplace
that the Jewish God of the Old Testament is the aloof judge,
who is mostly angry with the world and frightens his creatures
with his wrath and mighty deeds; whereas the God of the New
Testament is the comforting, forgiving, and loving Father.
As long ago as the middle of the second century the gnostic
Marcion conceived of the Jewish God as a kind of Lucifer who
was responsible for all evil on earth and with whom the
Christian God was at war. But it is original to see a modern
historian take up the cudgel on behalf of Marcion. We have
already heard Mr. Toynbee complain about the readmission
into Christianity of the "incongruous Israelitish concept and
service of the 'Jealous God' Yahweh." According to him, the
readmission was a matter of political expedience. Being engaged in a life-and-death struggle with the Caesaro-worship of
the Roman Empire, Christianity was unable to heed "Marcion's
prophetically warning voice." The God that is Love was of
not much good in such a conflict; one had to call in the God
that is Power. "Love had to cede the high command to Jealousy

if defeat was to be inflicted upon Caesar; and the restoration of peace through the Church's victory did not dissolve, but, on the contrary, confirmed, the incongruous association of Yahweh with Christ. . . ."[1]

It is intellectually embarrassing to have, at this late hour, to answer old Marcion. But since such notions were still being published in 1954, and even under the respectable imprint of the Oxford University Press, the statement of a Jewish point of view is obviously not superfluous.

Let us then, first, see what is the full truth, as revealed in the New Testament itself, concerning this "decisive new departure from Judaism" which was undertaken by Christianity "by recognizing and proclaiming that God is Love." Is the concept of God as found in the New Testament really free from jealousy, wrath, judgment, vengeance, and power? What of the "woe-unto-you" fulmination of Jesus against the Pharisees, the fanatical: "Ye serpents, ye generation of vipers, how can ye escape the damnation of hell?" The anger of the Lord is no less terrifying in the New Testament than it is in the Jewish Bible. No special scholarship is needed to compose a nice little Anthology of Wrath from the New Testament.

> O generation of vipers, who hath warned you to flee from the wrath to come? Bring forth therefore fruits meet for repentance: . . . Therefore every tree which bringeth not forth good fruit is hewn down, and cast into the fire.
>
> . . . but he that cometh after me is mightier than I . . . he shall baptize you with the Holy Ghost, and with fire: whose fan is in his hand, and he will thoroughly purge his floor, and gather his wheat into the garner; but he will burn up the chaff with unquenchable fire.
>
> The Son of man shall send forth his angels, and they shall gather out of his kingdom all things that offend, and them which do iniquity; and shall cast them into a furnace of fire: There shall be wailing and gnashing of teeth.
>
> Fear him, which after he hath killed hath power to cast into hell; yea, I say unto you, Fear him.

It is a fearful thing to fall into the hands of the living God.

For our God is a consuming fire.

For the wrath of God is revealed from heaven against all ungodliness and unrighteousness of men. . . .

What if God, willing to show his wrath, and to make his power known, endured with much longsuffering the vessels of wrath fitted to destruction.

. . . when the Lord Jesus shall be revealed from heaven with his mighty angels, in flaming fire taking vengeance on them that know not God, and obey not the gospel of our Lord Jesus Christ.

The same shall drink of the wine of the wrath of God, which is poured out without mixture into the cup of his indignation; and he shall be tormented with fire and brimstone in the presence of the holy angels, and in the presence of the Lamb.[2]

These quotations, gathered at random, are far from exhaustive. Let us now see what is the more complete truth about "the forbidding aspect of God as Power," the "incongruous Israelitish concept and service of the 'Jealous God' Yahweh." It seems that Mr. Toynbee himself does not feel comfortable in the strait jacket of his theory. In an annex he makes a partial withdrawal of what he teaches in Volumes VI and VII of his *Study*. There he concedes that it was not through Jesus that Jewish souls received the first intimation that God is Love. "The Mosaic presentation of Yahweh as a Jealous God, readily moved to anger, had been supplemented by the Prophetic presentation of Him as abounding in mercy and lovingkindness seven hundred years before the Christian Gospel was first preached."[3] Such a confession of itself invalidates the Toynbean position concerning the Israelitish Jealous God. But it is noteworthy that Mr. Toynbee can find no more adequate phrase to describe the Prophetic presentation of God than "abounding in mercy and lovingkindness"—which phrase is itself Mosaic. It was Moses to whom God revealed Himself as: "The Lord, the Lord God, merciful and gracious, long-suffering, and abundant in loving-kindness and truth; keeping mercy unto the thousandth generation, forgiving iniquity and transgression and sin."[4] The two commandments—"Thou shalt love the Lord thy God with all thy heart, and with all thy soul, and with all thy might" and "Thou shalt love thy neighbor as thyself"—are not part of the prophetic presentation but are found in the books of Moses, closely linked to the Jealous God; and yet Jesus said of them: "On these two commandments hang all the law and the prophets." There must be something essentially right about a "Jealous God" who admonishes His worshipers: "And if a stranger sojourn with thee in your land, ye shall not do him wrong. The stranger that sojourneth with you shall be unto you as the home-born among you, and *thou shalt love him as thyself. . .* "[5]

There is no need to enumerate further examples, to prove the same point; they are easily accessible to anyone who is prepared to read the Bible. The two aspects of God, as Power and as Love, are found side by side throughout the entire Bible. There may, indeed, be a problem here, but no less for Christian than for Jewish theology. Mr. Toynbee himself cannot avoid the issue. In the ninth volume of his *Study,* with the help of a "latter-day Western psychology" he finds verified the "intuition of Irenaeus" that the coexistence of two gods, morally antithetical to each other, is only apparent—"a mirage reflecting merely a diffraction of the unitary image of the One True God in the prismatic lens of an imperfect human spiritual vision."[6] Having in Volume VII taken the side of Marcion against the "incongruous Israelitish concept," now he takes the side of Irenaeus against Marcion, realizing that "Love is inseparable from the Almighty Power." In Volumes VI and VII, by ignoring the jealousy and judgment in the New Testament and the love and mercy in the Jewish Bible, Mr. Toynbee draws the contrast between the "forbidding aspect of God, as Power, which had been presented in the Mosaic matrix of Judaism" and the God that is Love. One is prepared to charge the blasphemy to Mr. Toynbee's own rather "imperfect spiritual vision." But what is one to think of the intellectual integrity of a historian who, having once made such an issue of the God of Love as "the heart of the Christian revelation," declares, without further explanation or apology to his readers: "As God is revealed in the Gospels, He is Love as well as Omnipotence . . ."?[7]!

2.

What has Judaism to say about the ambivalence of divine attributes which manifest Power as well as Love, Jealousy as well as Mercy, Judgment as well as Forgiveness? The fundamental mistake in Mr. Toynbee's theology is that he assumes that Biblical statements about God deal with the Divine Essence. Mr. Toynbee actually believes that when Moses sang of Him, "The Lord is a Man of War," Moses imagined God as being in essence a warrior. Our author might as well have said that, according to the primitive concept of the early Hebrews, God was a man. Similarly, he believes that the concept "God is Love" is a revelation about the Divine Nature proper. In truth, however, "God is Love" is no less an anthropomorphism than "God is Power" or "God is a Man of War." Love, Power, and War are notions of human experience; to attach any of them to the Divine Essence would be equally childish. Nor is there, on the basis of such crude anthropomorphism, any valid reason to assume that a God that is Love is incapable of Jealousy.

The final and conclusive truth about the Essence of God was revealed to Moses in the phrase: "I AM THAT I AM . . . Thus shalt thou say unto the children of Israel: I AM hath sent me unto you."[8] Since then, no one has been able to improve on the Mosaic insight. To this day it has represented the last word on the Nature of God. Pharisaic teaching drew the correct conclusions from it, by stating that one could not call God after His nature, but only after His deeds. Since these are manifold, the "names" of God, too, are many. When He judges the world, He is called Elohim; when He wages war on the wicked, He may be referred to as Zebaoth; and when He treats His world with mercy, His appellation is Hashem.[9] The Divine Attributes are not the result of abstract reasoning about God, but the crystallization of religious experience, in so far as man is able to relate it to God. They do not reveal the Essence of God, which is unfathomable, but speak only of man's encounter with God. In this encounter the basic element is a sense of awe, of an Almighty Presence, of a transcendental Reality that is essentially different from man and beside Whom man is threatened with disappearance into Nothingness. Without such a sense of the overwhelming Otherness of God there is no religion. It is to this experience that the "consuming Fire" and the terrible power of God, even His Wrath, attempt to give expression in man's inadequate language.[10] One cannot go hobnobbing with the Almighty or run to Him at any time and sit on His knee as if He were dear old Dad. Even in Christian tradition, in his hour of supreme test, Jesus could not suppress the exclamation: "Eli, Eli! Lama azabtani"—"My God, my God! Why hast Thou forsaken me!"

However, although the experience of fear is the precondition of religion, it is insufficient for the religious encounter. In order to meet God, man must be able to "stand up" to Him, as it were; he must be able to face the *Mysterium Tremendum*. Man, who is completely dependent on his Maker, must possess a measure of independence, of self-owned personality, if he is to face his Maker. But it is the Love of God for him that alone can protect him against the Terror of the Almighty. The Terror is unavoidable, for "I Am that I Am" and man is what he is; the Love of God grants him the strength to be able to bear the encounter with God. Power and Love act together in order to make religious life possible. Overwhelmed by the Transcendence of God, Abraham cannot but exclaim: ". . . who am I but dust and ashes." However, this heap of "but dust and ashes," lifted up by the Love of God, owns his soul in moral independence so as to be able to plead the cause of Sodom and Gomorrah in the fearfully bold words: "That be far from Thee to do after this manner, to slay the righteous with the wicked, that so the righteous should be as the wicked; that be far from Thee; shall not the Judge of all the earth do justly?"[11]

The concept of "God the Father" is deeply embedded in Judaism. "Our Father that art in Heaven" was not a Christian discovery; Jesus learned it from the Pharisees. "Father of

Mercy" is a characteristically Jewish appellation for God, which Jews have been using through the ages and which of course has its origin in the verse of the Psalms: "Like as a father hath compassion upon his children, so hath the Lord compassion upon them that fear Him."[12] For Judaism, however, God is Father and King, Father and Lord Creator, as it is written: "Is not He thy father that hath gotten thee? Hath He not made thee, and established thee?"[13] The great Rabbi Akiba, who sought a martyr's death during the Hadrianic persecutions, interpreted the "Song of Songs"—to him the holiest of all "Songs"—as a symbolic expression of the mystery of Love between God and Israel; yet at a time of crisis he did not intercede with God by the appellation "Beloved," but prayed: "Our Father, Our King! Thou art our Father. Our Father, Our King! We have no other King but Thee."[14] And to this day, when on Rosh Hashana and Yom Kippur, the holiest days of the Jewish year, Israel pleads with God, it addresses itself to "Our Father, Our King!"

One of the great Pharisaic teachers of the third century C.E., living about a hundred years after Rabbi Akiba, Rabbi Johanan, expressed the antithetical nature of God's relationship to man in the following words:

In every passage where thou findest the greatness of God mentioned, there thou findest also his humility. . . It is written in the Law: "For the Lord your God, he is God of gods, and Lord of lords, the great, mighty and revered God, who regardeth no persons, nor taketh a bribe." And it is written afterwards, "He doth execute the judgment of the fatherless and widow, and loveth the stranger, in giving him food and raiment." It is repeated in the Prophets, as it is written, "For thus saith the high and lofty One that inhabiteth eternity, and whose name is holy, I dwell in the High and holy places, with him also that is of a contrite and humble spirit, to revive the spirit of the humble, and to revive the heart of the contrite ones." It is a third time stated in the Writings, "Sing unto God, sing praises to his name: Extol ye him that rideth upon the heavens..., and rejoice before him." And it is written afterwards, "A Father of the fatherless, and a judge of the widows, is God in his holy habitation."[15]

The Aloofness, the Transcendence, which are not separable from the basic religious experience, are forced into humanly bearable dimensions by God's Humility. Without that Humility, which cares for man and sustains him, no relationship between God and His Creation would be possible.

The ambivalence of the encounter between Creator and creature is reflected in Judaism's evaluation of man. It found its classical expression in the words of the Psalmist:

What is man, that Thou art mindful of him?
And the son of man that Thou thinkest of him?
Yet Thou hast made him but little lower than the angels,
And hast crowned him with glory and honor.[16]

God's crushing Infinitude turns man into nothingness, God's sustaining Humility crowns him with glory; the heap of dust and ashes was granted the dignity of bearing the "Image." Or, as Rabbi Akiba put it: "Beloved is man, for he was created in the image of God; abundant love was made known to him that he was created in the image of God."[17] Man is not invaluable but he is not without value. He is not essentially good but, thanks to the Love of God for him, he is capable of goodness. He is, therefore, a responsible creature and the Love of God is the source of his responsibility. The Jealousy of God is the corollary to man's moral dignity. The idea of the Jealous God is the manifestation of the moral and religious imperative addressed to man. It means that, having established man's dignity, He takes man seriously; He deems him worthy of rendering an account of what he does with his life.

It was here that Christianity parted company with Judaism. The core of the Pauline teaching was that "man sold under sin" was incapable of saving himself by his own exertions. The Law of God was a burden too heavy for him to bear; the Love of God freed man from the slavery of the Law. According to Pauline teaching, Law and Sin came first and Love entered the world in order to redeem man from both. Judaism believes that Love was at the beginning. Or, as the Pharisees taught, from the beginning the world was created with nothing but loving-kindness.[18] The Love of God made man great enough to enable him to seek his salvation in a life in accordance with the Law of God. The Law is a sign of God's confidence in man. Man *can* follow it and the responsibility is his. From the Jewish point of view the greater emphasis in Christianity on Love and Grace is not the mark of a higher concept of the Divinity but rather the manifestation of a pessimistic evaluation of the inherent possibilities of man. If, as the result of an Original Sin, man's nature is corrupt, if he can do no good by his own strength, then of course the rigor of a code of "Thou Shalt" is meaningless. If, however—as Judaism teaches —man has been equipped by the Love of God with the potential for continuous moral and spiritual increase, then the Law expresses the idea that God does consider and regard man. Far from seeing a burden in the Law, Judaism is elated by it. For:

> The law of the Lord is perfect, restoring the soul;
> The testimony of the Lord is sure, making wise the simple.
> The precepts of the Lord are right, rejoicing the heart;
> The commandment of the Lord is pure, enlightening the eyes.
> The fear of the Lord is clean, enduring for ever;
> The ordinances of the Lord are true, they are righteous altogether;
> More to be desired are they than gold, yea, than much fine gold,
> Sweeter also than honey and the honeycomb.[19]

In Jewish teaching it was the Love of God that bestowed the Law on Israel.[20] Of course, where there is a Law, there is also Judgment and Jealousness. However, Anger and Love, Punishment and Mercy, both carry the message that God does care for man, that He is mindful of His creature. By Judgment alone, man cannot stand; by Forgiveness alone, man will not advance. Through Judgment and Forgiveness the Kingly Father calls man to his salvation. In innumerable variations, the thought is consistently expressed in Jewish teaching through the ages. It is the meaning of the words: "And thou shalt consider in thy heart, that, as a man chasteneth his son, so the Lord thy God chasteneth thee." Rabbi Eleazar, a disciple of Rabbi Johanan, whom we have quoted concerning the antinomy in the encounter with God, expressed it by saying: "Even in the moment of His Anger, the Holy One, blessed be He, remembers His Mercy."[21]

2. JEWISH UNIVERSALISM AND THE "CHOSEN PEOPLE"

1.

We noted that Mr. Toynbee attributed the jealousy and intolerance of the Israelitish God to the absence of a universal vision. It was the element of universality that distinguished Christianity from the beginning, the ideal that Jewry, blinded by the delusion of being God's Chosen People, rejected.

It is not a very flattering commentary on the spiritual situation of our times that in this mid-twentieth century it still seems necessary to argue the fallacy of such hackneyed distortions of the truth. The God who created heaven and earth, whom Moses called "God of the spirits of all flesh," of whom Isaiah said that "He stretcheth forth the heavens and layeth the foundation of the earth, and formeth the spirit of man within"—how could He be less than the Universal Creator? Even an Israelitish housewife in "the hill-country of Ephraim," at the time of the Judges in Jewish history, had the notion that "there is none beside Thee. . . . For the pillars of the earth are the Lord's, and He hath set the world upon them!" Innumerable passages crowd one's mind as one ponders on the subject; but few in the religious literature of mankind convey a more convincing impression of the all-embracing scope of man's belief in God than the inspired words of Psalm 96:

Let the heavens be glad, and let the earth rejoice;
Let the sea roar, and all that is therein;

Then shall all the trees of the wood sing for joy;
Before the Lord, for He is come;
For He is come to judge the earth;
He will judge the world with righteousness,
And the peoples in His faithfulness.

The idea of the universal God has its corollary in the essential oneness of the universal creation. It finds expression in the passage just quoted—in the joyous participation of the entire creation in the righteous judgment of the peoples and the world. No one is excluded from the providential care of the Universal Creator. Where has the thought found nobler expression than in the glorious Psalm 145? It is sufficient to recall only a few of the better-known verses:

The Lord is gracious, and full of compassion;
Slow to anger, and of great mercy.
The Lord is good to all;
And His tender mercies are over all His works.

. . . .

The Lord upholdeth all that fall,
And raiseth up all those that are bowed down.
The eyes of all wait for Thee,
And Thou givest them their food in due season.
Thou openest Thy hand,
And satisfiest every living thing with favour.

. . . .

The Lord is nigh unto all them that call upon Him,
To all that call upon Him in truth.

We have quoted the vision of eternal peace and universal reconciliation that the Jewish prophet Isaiah bequeathed to mankind four centuries before Alexander the Great, whose spirit was—according to Mr. Toynbee—the inspiration of Jesus. Of even greater significance, however, is the fact that Isaiah not only sees the vision of a peacefully united mankind as an abstract hope but applies it to the contemporary political scene, the "hereditary" enemies of Judah and Israel. At a time when Judah was torn between Assyria and Egypt, Isaiah was

63

looking forward to the day when Israel shall "be the third with Egypt and with Assyria, a blessing in the midst of the earth; for that the Lord of hosts hath blessed him saying: Blessed be Egypt my people and Assyria the work of My hands, and Israel Mine inheritance."[22]

We shall see how the Biblical tradition of Judaic universalism was maintained and further elaborated by the Pharisees, the only authentic successors to the prophets in Israel. In the meantime let their position be indicated by one of the basic Pharisaic concepts. To the question, Why did God create only *one* man to start off the history of the human race and not more than one, they gave the answer: It was done for the sake of the peace of mankind; that no man should rightly be able to say to his fellow: My father is greater than your father.[23] Mankind's descent from one Adam establishes the essential equality of the human race. The Pharisaic teaching represents the most universal application of the significance of the words of Malachi: "Have we not all one father? Hath not one God created us?"[24]

2.

The massive proof of Judaic universalism, however, seems to be vitiated by the concept of the Chosen People. Yet, the two apparently antithetical ideas dwell peacefully side by side in the Bible. The Universal Creator, Sustainer, and Savior, the Universal Creation, and the ideal of Universal Peace, toward which all history is moving, are proclaimed together with the concept that Israel is a "peculiar" people. Isaiah calls Israel the "Holy Seed"; Jeremiah, "the Lord's Hallowed Portion."[25] And, indeed, a less partisan approach to the subject will reveal that the Chosen People idea, far from excluding universalism, actually presupposes it. That God has chosen Israel "to be His own treasure out of all peoples that are upon the face of the earth"[26] is of significance only if He could have chosen any other nation likewise. If He could have taken unto Himself any other of the families of the earth and yet took Israel, then indeed there was a choice. But only the God of all mankind has the possibility of such a choice before Him. The very notion of such a choice also presupposes the concept of mankind; before the choice, Israel is one among the nations that are under the scrutiny of the Universal Creator. It is from the *midst of mankind* that Israel was singled out.[27] Since, however, the "God of the Spirit of all Flesh" was associated with justice and righteousness, mercy and loving-kindness, the election of Israel could not have meant the abandonment by the Almighty of the rest of the world. The just and gracious God cannot give up His responsibility toward any part of His creation. Therefore, the essence of the idea of a Chosen People derives from the notion that the Father of all mankind single out one of His children for some reason or for some purpose. Eliminate the concept of a Universal Creator, concerned about His entire creation, remove the recognition of mankind rightly claiming the attention of its Maker, and to be a Chosen People becomes an utterly uninteresting, lame, and lifeless proposition. The Bible calls Israel God's "First born son";[28] the very idea implies the concept of a family, with God as the Father and the nations of the earth as His Children, and brothers to each other through His Fatherhood.

Probably the most significant aspect of the Chosen People concept is, however, usually overlooked. The notion does not belong in the realm either of theology or of metaphysics. Jewish theology, often described as the theology of ethical monotheism, contains no concept to justify the assumption of a Chosen People; nor is there anything in the principles of a metaphysics corresponding to Jewish monotheism that may lead to the Chosen People idea. The idea indicates an event in history, not a theoretical principle of faith or philosophy. If, for example, one should accept the definition of dogma as a "proposition having metaphysical significance,"[29] the belief in being a Chosen People could not even be considered a religious dogma of Judaism. Whether God did or did not elect Israel has no consequence whatever for Israel's interpretation either of the Nature of God or of Reality. It is the same God and the same Universe whether Israel is chosen or rejected. Judaism's faith in God never depended on God's treatment of Israel, "for I the Lord change not."[30]

That God chose Israel means, first of all, that an actual encounter took place between Him and Israel. The encounter between man and God, in whatever way one explains it, is of the essence of religion. The people of Israel went through a number of experiences that carried within themselves the certitude that God was addressing Himself to them. This "meeting" between Israel and God granted them the unique insight that He was a "Living" God.[31] The "Living" God is "present" in every original religious experience, and it is He who puts into the mouth of man the appellation adequate for the experience. "Almighty God," "Father of all Men," "Gracious and Beneficent Creator"—they sound rather dignified and they are well suited for the decorous invocation of the Almighty on all kinds of official occasions; but with "acute" religion they have little to do. The man who feels that he is in the presence of God, who in an actual experience faces God, will most naturally address himself not to the "Creator of the Universe" but to "My God," "My Light," "My Help," "My Salvation." In the live encounter with God, and even only on its mere fringes, God is "personalized"; He becomes man's very own. All religious literature, referring to a genuine religious experience, testifies to this. "My God" is the natural exclamation of the human soul when it seeks or senses the Presence of the "Living" God. However, the "My God" of the individual experience becomes "Our God" in the collective experience of a people. In the individual encounter God is "egotized," in the collective one He is "tribalized." In both cases the human being *individually* takes "possession" of God. Still recalling the original encounter, people often use the term "My God," even though the experience has passed; similarly, the "Our God" of the Jewish encounters is, at times, reflected in the less "personalized" form of the "God of Israel." "My God," "Our God," "God of Israel"—all these forms of appellation are philosophical and metaphysical monstrosities, yet they are related to the very essence of the original religious experience; they are manifestations of the intensity of the charge communicated to the soul of man.

The Jewish concept of the Chosen People goes beyond this

position. The original experiences of the encounter are short, quickly passing; the covenant between God and Israel is permanent. It is, however, on the occasion of the actual encounter that the covenant is made; it still indicates an event in history. The covenant links encounter with encounter and, thus, turns the history of Israel into a people's life with God. "Our God" becomes "Our God and the God of our Fathers." Whatever Israel does or does not do is adjudged in the context of the covenant; all Jewish behavior becomes a form of intercourse with God. Thus the covenant grants no privileges but is the source of greater demands and heightened responsibility. From the outset it is made clear to Israel that it may expect no preferential treatment, and everything is done to warn it against conceit. The most frightening of retributions in the Bible are reserved for Israel. As to the land that was to become theirs, it is impressed upon them: "Know therefore that it is not for thy righteousness that the Lord thy God giveth thee this good land to possess it; for thou art a stiffnecked people." Amos expresses the main burden of the entire prophetic message to Israel when he reveals to the people the word of God saying: "You only have I known of all the families of the earth; therefore I will visit upon you all your iniquities."[32]

We may now be able to appreciate that the Chosen People idea not only may dwell amicably side by side with Jewish universalism but, in fact, helps to sustain it. Since Israel is a "peculiar people" not by virtue of a metaphysical or a theological truth but as the result of an actual revelation of God, the obligations that follow from the encounter are not binding on any one except on Israel itself. Judaism knows of the "Seven Commandments of the Sons of Noah," which are the responsibility of all mankind and which may be understood as the principles of a universal ethical monotheism. But what the Torah contains beyond these Commandments is enjoined only on Israel. The covenant with God excludes the rest of mankind from the *duty* to observe and to practice the precepts of the covenant. The precepts and the laws have intellectual and ethical validity in general; but they are an obligation only for Israel, to whom they were revealed as the command of God.

Gentiles are free to accept them, if convinced of their truth; since, however, a command is authoritative only in so far as it is actually uttered as such, it is meaningless to enforce the covenant on those with whom it has not been concluded. The Pharisees were able to declare without equivocation that any ulterior motive for the acceptance of Judaism, be it love or fear of man, hope for material reward or dread of loss, invalidates the conversion of a Gentile. "Rabbi Yehudah and Rabbi Nehemia said: All those Gentiles that became converted to Judaism in the days of Mordecai and Esther are no proselytes, for it is said of them: 'And many from among the peoples of the land became Jews; for the fear of the Jews was fallen upon them'; but those who do not accept Judaism for the sake of heaven are no proselytes."[33] A minor can be admitted to conversion only if offered for it by his father or, if the father is dead, by the mother. In either case, the conversion is only conditional: when a proselytized minor comes of age, it is his right to revoke the consent of his parental guardian. This has been Judaic teaching through the ages.[34] At all times in the history of Judaism, any enforced conversion was contrary to the law and invalid. The Christian dictum, "Compel them to enter" (*coge intrare*), is inconceivable within the matrix of Judaism.

Judaism does not encourage proselytism because the proselyte accepts a great many duties and responsibilities which previously were not incumbent upon him and concerning which, therefore, he could never lose his "innocence." A Gentile, who does not practice Judaism, is not a sinner; a proselyte, by becoming a Jew, exposes himself to the wider possibilities of failure and sin. At the same time, Judaism looks with admiration and respect on the "Ger Tsedek," the "Righteous Proselyte," who becomes a Jew out of inner conviction. His prototype is the Patriarch Abraham, who found his way to God by free choice and personal faith. The proselyte of conviction is "beloved by God," he is "great in the sight of God," for he becomes a Jew for the sake of God. "Happy is every one that feareth the Lord, that walketh in His ways": the verse is applied to him.[35]

It may now be of some interest to recall one of the major

points made by Mr. Toynbee against Judaism. Having ignored
the existence of the strong peace party in Jerusalem, which was
led by the Pharisees, and having rejected the two forms of
"Jewish" response, "Herodianism" and "Zealotism," he proceeds to describe the only successful response as that of "Evangelism," which transcends the petty boundaries of a mundane
struggle between one civilization and another by means of a
universal faith. His text is the well-known phrase of the
Christian apostle Paul: "There is neither Jew nor Greek, there
is neither bond nor free, there is neither male nor female; for
ye are all one in Christ Jesus."[36] Being ignorant of almost all
matters concerning Judaism, Toynbee did not realize that, if
we had not known it already, these words by themselves would
convincingly reveal the Pharisaic past of the Christian apostle.
They are orthodox Judaic teaching, removed from their original context and transferred to the Christian frame of reference. The tenor of universalism in the Pauline maxim is
found, for example, in the Midrash, where it is said: "The
Holy One, blessed be He, does not reject any one of His creatures but is ready to receive them all. The gates remain open
at all times and all who wish to enter may come and enter."[37]
Not only in thought but also in mode of expression has Paul
been preceded by his Pharisaic teachers. Commenting on the
verse of the Psalms, quoted above, "Happy is every one that
feareth the Lord," the anonymous Pharisaic tradition explained: It is not said, "Happy are the Israelites," nor, "Happy
are the Priests and Levites," but, "Happy are all they that fear
the Lord": the reference is to the proselytes who fear God.
They are to be adjudged happy just as Moses said of Israel:
"Happy art thou, O Israel!" It is for this reason that the
Psalmist included both in one phrase: "Happy is *everyone* that
feareth the Lord."[38] In the same vein of Pharisaic teaching,
and most probably having it at the back of his mind, Rabbi
Meir of the second century c.e. taught: "How does one know
that even a Gentile who occupies himself with the Torah is like
unto the High Priest? Says the Bible of the precepts of the
Torah: . . . 'which if a man do, he shall live by them. . . .' Note
that it is not said, 'which priests, Levites, or Israelites do' but,

'which a man do.' You should derive from it that any man, even a Gentile, if he occupies himself with the Torah is like unto the High Priest."[39] Nothing could be easier than to paraphrase these Pharisaic traditions by saying: There is neither Jew nor Gentile, there is neither bond nor free, there is neither male nor female; for ye are all one in the fear of the Lord.[40] In Pauline doctrine the "fear of the Lord" or the Torah was replaced by faith in Jesus. The reference to Jesus is the only Pauline innovation here; the concept of universalism is good old Judaism.

In view of the perennial distortions and falsifications to which Judaic universalism is still exposed at the hand of Christian scholarship, let it be said for once that by placing it in the Christian context Paul actually narrowed the scope of the universalism of his teachers. It did not enter the minds of the Pharisees that Gentiles could find no salvation without accepting the Torah. If Gentiles occupied themselves with the Torah they might earn a distinction, but it was not considered necessary to earn such a distinction in order to be saved. Judaism does not maintain that it is the sole repository of man's salvation. Judaism is the only way of salvation for Jews. As to the rest of mankind it was stated: "The righteous of all the nations have a share in the World-to-come."[41] Even more striking is the interpretation placed on the words of the Psalmist: "Let Thy priests be clothed with righteousness. . . ." It is explained that the reference is to the "righteous among the nations; for they are the priests of the Holy One, blessed be He, in this world."[42] Paul did say, "For ye are all children of God" —and was only repeating what had been said before him by the prophets and teachers in Israel—but he qualified it by adding, ". . . by faith in Christ Jesus."[43] According to him all men are children of God conditionally—provided that they believe in Jesus. This of course was Christian teaching from the beginning. Jesus himself insisted that "No man cometh unto the Father but by me"[44]; and the utterance remained a cornerstone in the teachings of the apostles. The Church Fathers clung to it when, in their own way, they asserted that there was no salvation outside the Church. All men are equally precious children of God—if they believe in Christ Jesus; but for those who do not believe there is but "the wine of wrath of God," torments by "fire and brimstone," and eternal damnation. With all due respect to Christianity, this is universalism with strings attached to it; it would be more correct to refer to it as religious totalitarianism.

Of course, the issue should not be approached with the childish Toynbean concept of Gentleness versus Violence, or of Tolerance versus Intolerance. Christianity's religious totalitarianism is the inevitable logical consequence of the nature of its universalism. The central Christian dogma maintains that in Jesus God gave Himself to the *World* in order to save *all mankind*. We may call it a dogma since the proposition does have "metaphysical significance." It not only describes an event but reveals something about the essence of God and the nature of Reality. It is for this reason that the Christian revelation is universal; it is directed to every living thing. The New Covenant of faith is made with the world at large, whereas the Old Covenant of the "Law" was made with Israel alone. But just on account of this, whereas the Old Covenant placed the responsibility for the "Law" on the Jews alone, the New Covenant demands that all men believe. In Judaism, he who breaks the "Law" is a sinner, but only Jews can break it; from the point of view of Christianity, he who does not believe in the "Son of God" is the sinner and all men are called upon to believe. Because Israel is the "Chosen People," salvation cannot be denied to the Gentiles, who are outside the Covenant; because Christian revelation is "universalistic," all those who are outside the Church are against it and he who does not believe is lost.

One might pursue the reason for this difference one step further. We have already observed that the Pauline replacement of the "Law" by "Faith" was due to the fact that man was considered incapable of doing right through his own exertions. He can only be saved from the bondage of Sin through faith. Judaism, on the other hand, teaches that from the beginning God in His Love equipped man with the freedom to strive for what is right as well as with the ability to do it. It is for man to realize his potentialities. In Christianity, as a result of Original Sin, all human nature is corrupt and in need of salvation; in Judaism, because of the original Act of Creation by God, all human nature is capable of goodness and is in need of self-realization. In Christianity a man comes to God only by faith, and therefore any other religion and any other way of life that do not make the faith in "Christ Jesus" their own must be rejected. In Judaism, however, every man comes to God by his own exertions—by making use of his inherent abilities as they have been granted to him, by doing what is right much more than by believing in this or that dogma. Therefore, in view of the Covenant, there is no salvation for the Jew outside Judaism; having encountered God, the Jew has no escape from Him. But on account of the inherent, God-granted potentialities of human nature the possibility for the Encounter remains open all the time for every human being. "The righteous of all the nations have a share in the World-to-come."

3.

This is not the place to pursue the theological and philosophical ramifications of the differences which are implied in the basic Christian and Jewish positions. We trust, however, that it has become clear that the Chosen People idea has prevented the universalistic element in Jewish monotheism from turning Judaism into a crusading religion, whereas the very claim of Christianity to "catholicity," to bring the sole repository of all human salvation, compels it to adopt a totalitarian attitude in matters of religious faith.

As regards Christianity, Toynbee himself explicitly concedes the point. Being a historian, he attempts to be objective toward the three non-Christian living Higher Religions. He struggles bravely with "the crux for a Christian historian," trying to correct the bias inherent in "the historical accidents of his birth and upbringing." He reaches the conclusion that the four living Higher Religions, Christianity, Islam, Buddhism, and Hinduism, correspond to four basic psychological types and their spiritual needs. They are variations on one single theme and the components of a heavenly harmony. At the same time, he cannot but agree that his critique is right in saying that this solution of the problem is not in "Christian terms." He concludes by stating: "In denying that other religions may be God's chosen and sufficient channels for revealing Himself to some human souls, it seems to me to be guilty of blasphemy. If it is inadmissible to call oneself a Christian without holding these tenets, then I am not entitled to call myself a Christian. . . ."[45] In vain does Toynbee suggest that there might be a slight possibility that the word "Christian" is not to be confined to the sense in which the word has been used in the Church's "own authoritative statements of its position." Not only "historically and juridically" but even more theologically the Christian Church is a more trustworthy authority on Christianity than Mr. Toynbee. There is no getting away from it: if it is true, as Jesus taught, that "No man cometh to the Father but by me," then there is indeed only one channel open for God's revelation to man, namely, Christianity.

Mr. Toynbee might have found it much easier to justify the possibility of various channels of divine revelation, without breaking with an ancestral tradition, had he been a Jew. Exactly such a possibility was asserted five centuries before Jesus by the Jewish prophet Malachi, when he proclaimed: "For from the rising of the sun even unto the going down of the same My name is great among the nations; and in every place offerings are presented unto My name . . . for My name is great among the nations, saith the Lord of hosts."[46] No doubt the prophet meant that, notwithstanding the election of Israel, the avenues of approach to God were not closed to the rest of mankind. We have already noticed that the Pharisees, in their own way, reaffirmed the same position. But what a shock it would be for Mr. Toynbee to learn that, even in the manner of expressing his theory, he is practically imitating the Pharisaic phraseology. Commenting on the words of the Psalmist, "The voice of the Lord through power"[47] the rabbis in the Midrash explained:

It is not said: "The voice of the Lord through His power"; for had He addressed Himself to Man with His own power, the world could not have survived the Voice. But "The voice of the Lord with power" is indefinite, for it refers to every one of those who heard God's voice. Each of them received the Voice in accordance with his or her own power; the young ones and the old ones, men and women, children and infants, even Moses himself, each of them heard the Voice commensurately with his or her personal receptive capacity. Said the Holy One, blessed be He, to Israel: "Do not think that because you have heard many voices there must be many gods; but know that I am the Lord thy God."[48]

Since God's essence is inapproachable by man, all Divine Revelation is relative to man; even the same Word is received differently by different people. God gives Himself to every human being in accordance with his specific individuality. But the man-conditioned and man-necessitated variety of Revelation originates but from one source, the unconditioned and undifferentiated and absolute truth that "I Am that I Am." Mr. Toynbee does not know Judaism; yet he sounded—unwittingly —like a latter-day disciple of the Pharisees when he wrote: "Uniformity is not possible in Man's approach to the One True God because Human Nature is stamped with the fruitful diversity that is a hall-mark of God's creative work. . . . God's ineffable brightness is never revealed, utterly unveiled, to the naked eye of Man's frail spirit in its passage through This World. 'The true light . . .' has to be received by every creature according to the particular lights with which the Creator has endowed it."[49] As Mr. Toynbee himself agrees, this cannot be maintained in terms of Christianity; but it does sound like a paraphrasing of Pharisaic teaching in the literary tradition of the West. Salvation, according to Judaism, is a gradual process in history that depends on man's realization of his God-given potentialities and in which every human being may participate. In Christianity, however, salvation is a single act of grace, which is outside history; it is instantaneous and complete. One is either saved by faith or damned without it.[50]

Exclusiveness is of the very essence of the Christian premise;

74

from this inevitably follows the rejection of the thought that there could be any other possible avenue of approach to God outside Christianity. This concept has—as is well known—found rather bizarre expression in Christian theology and philosophy. Augustine, for instance, maintained that even infants, if they die unbaptized, are given over to eternal damnation. Dante relegates the virtuous heathens, even though they lived before Jesus, to Limbo. They are condemned to an eternity "of untormented sadness." And as to the torments of the sinners and the horrifying sadism perpetrated against them, the poet instructs us: "There is no place for pity here. Who is more arrogant within his soul, who is more impious than one who dares to sorrow, at God's Judgment?"[51] According to Thomas Aquinas, known as the Angelic Doctor, "to witness the sufferings of the damned adds to the felicity of the redeemed in Heaven."[52]

One cannot help comparing with such manifestations of "universalism" the Pharisaic thought embodied in a Talmudical parable. It is said: "Rabbi Samuel, the Son of Nahman, said in the name of Rabbi Jonathan . . . At the time of the destruction of the Egyptians in the Red Sea, the administering angels were about to chant their appointed hymn before the Holy One, blessed be He. Said to them the Holy One, blessed be He: the works of My hands are drowning in the sea and you dare sing My praise before Me!"[53] History is not a Sunday school; there is guilt in it and judgment too. But all judgment is tragedy, even if it be as well deserved as Jews believed the judgment of ancient Egypt to be. Judgment is a cosmic tragedy, for it is always on "the works of His hands" that it is executed.

3. JEWS, GENTILES, AND JESUS

1.

Nothing could be more wrong than Toynbee's suggestion that Jewry's negative attitude to the Gentiles was the reason for its rejection of the Christian gospel of universal salvation. There were no mundane advantages implied in being God's

75

Chosen People, and no one was more clear about this than the Jews themselves. As to the spiritual privilege of having duties and responsibilities, in addition to the "Seven Commandments" of a basic universal and "natural" religion considered to be incumbent on all mankind, no man was excluded from it. For the Jews there was no escape; for the Gentiles there was freedom to enter. The Covenant was exclusive in so far as it imposed the added responsibility on Jews alone; the promise that it contained was offered to all who were prepared to join in the Covenant. But Judaism was never possessed of intense missionary zeal, because its tenets of a Universal God and a universal humanity did not let it indulge in the spiritual conceit that it alone was the dispenser of all human salvation on earth.

It shows a complete lack of understanding of the Jewish position to write, as Toynbee does, that "pious Jews . . . execrated the Christians as libertines who had betrayed the faith of their fathers by admitting Gentiles into religious communion with Christian Jews and by exempting these uncircumcised proselytes from the duty of observing the Mosaic Law."[54] As we saw, "the duty of observing the Mosaic Law" existed only for Jews; there was, therefore, never any need to exempt Gentiles from it. On the other hand, there was no Judaism—nor can there be one—without "the duty of observing the Mosaic Law." To accept Judaism without accepting the Mosaic Law is a contradiction in terms. The "uncircumcised proselytes" were not proselytes to Judaism but to the New Faith; the issue in point had nothing to do with Jewry's attitude to Gentiles but to the New Faith. Not the association with Gentiles as such was "execrated" but the nature of the "religious communion" in which it took place. Even if Christianity had been preached to Jews alone, as perhaps was the original intention of Jesus,[55] Jewry's attitude to it would not have been different. From the Jewish point of view, Christianity was a new religion. The concepts of a Son of God and a God Incarnate were, as Toynbee convincingly shows, of heathen origin; the replacement of the duty to observe the Mosaic Law by faith in a "Son of God" was a complete rejection of Judaism. People may of course disagree with the Jewish interpretation of Judaism; but it is the mark of a little soul not to be able to acknowledge that Jewry, in its rejection of the claims on behalf of Jesus, was motivated by its religious conscience and by devotion to the truth as it saw it.

2.

We have also seen that there was no foundation for the Toynbean assertion that, having first made a radical new departure from Judaism by maintaining that "God is Love," Christianity—for the sake of expedience—"readmitted" the Israelitish Jealous God. There was no new departure either as regards the Love or the Jealousy of God. Both are eminently present in the Jewish Bible as well as in the New Testament. All Toynbean references to "Judaic" intolerance and fanaticism are the figments of a biased imagination. It would seem that, intolerance and fanaticism might find a more conducive psychological climate within the uncompromisingly exclusive ecumenicalism of Christianity than within Judaism, whose theological and metaphysical universalism is tempered by the concept of a "peculiar people."

We may now be equipped to evaluate the Toynbean proposition that Maccabean religious fanaticism, inherited by Christendom, was responsible for the specifically Christian brand of anti-Semitism. In our analysis of the idea in the context of Toynbeanism, we were able to show that even there it could be given an air of plausibility only by means of intellectual charlatanry and literary trickery. We shall now consider the idea from the standpoint of Judaism, as well as in the context of the history of Western Christendom, as described by Mr. Toynbee himself.

In our survey of the significance of the Maccabean and Hasmonean period, we showed that the forcible conversion of some Gentiles in Galilee and Idumea—the basis of the Toynbean contention—was undertaken not by the Maccabees but by two despotic Hasmonean princes, who were at war with their own people and with its recognized representatives, the Pharisees, the only authentic teachers of Judaism. Furthermore, since

Judaism never recognized any forcible conversion, the act of the Hasmonean princes was illegal and their proselytization invalid.[56] The two princes were Hellenized Sadducees, and it is strange that Christianity should have followed their example more than the teachings of its own founder.

However, in the context of the general history of Western Christendom, the "vein of hidden irony" in Christian anti-Semitism makes still less sense. As is well known, in the long history of the West anti-Semitism is only one specific manifestation of barbarism and criminality. There is much more to be explained than anti-Semitism. Toynbee attempts to offer a systematic classification of Western criminality. It would appear that religious persecution is the least heinous expression of inhumanity of which Western Christendom has been guilty. The treatment of various "underdogs" as barbarians, as "natives," and as inferior races are the other, successively more serious manifestations of Western inhumanity. The extermination of entire races by the Western colonizing powers, the unspeakable crimes of the slave raids in Africa, the barbarous treatment and exploitation of colored and native populations, the social injustices, the wars of greed and plunder—all these call for explanation. Toynbee himself cannot overlook the fact that more often than not the colonizing pioneer from the West acted "on the assumption that he is morally at liberty to pursue his own best interests as he sees them, without being called upon to treat the Natives as anything but wolves to be exterminated or sheep to be shorn." From Toynbee's presentation it arises clearly that the Nazis were not the original discoverers of a policy and behavior based on a theory of racial supremacy. Of the English-speaking Protestant pioneers, the historian says that these "West European Lords of Creation had been apt to clinch their assertion of their victims' political and academic nullity by going on to stigmatize these 'Natives' as the spawn of 'inferior races.' "[57] One is rather grateful to Toynbee that these —in his own opinion—more ghastly crimes of the West he ascribes not to Maccabeanism or the Judaic element in the Christian ethos but to the inherent corruption of human nature, i.e., to Original Sin.[58] In other words, Mr. Toynbee maintains

78

that the crime of Christian anti-Semitism is due to the Judaic influence in Christianity, whereas the other crimes, surpassing anti-Semitism in volume and intensity, are due to human nature. Since, however, the corruptness of human nature must be assumed to explain the criminality of Western man, what reason is there to believe that it was not also responsible for the barbarous persecution of the Jews? Surely Mr. Toynbee's theory offends against the elementary requirements of what is called in scientific research the "Simplicity Postulate"[59] and which since time immemorial has been a basic principle of logical induction. One should concede that his ability of sound reasoning lets him down chiefly when the subjects he discusses are directly related to Judaism or Jewry; otherwise, he is quite capable of logical thinking. For instance, he knows very well that fanaticism is fanaticism—and that it has one and the same source in human nature, no matter in which specific garb it may make itself felt. Discussing the wars of religion in Europe in their relationship to the wars of nationality which followed—which is of course a subject not directly connected with Jews—Toynbee acknowledges that "in our modern Western World the spirit of religious fanaticism and the spirit of national fanaticism are manifestly one and the same evil passion masquerading under a superficial diversity of interest and objective."[60] Indeed, the same evil passion, the same Original Sin, explains a great variety of the manifestations of human barbarism, including that of anti-Semitism. As an English psychologist has pointed out, most people do not act in accordance with principles and ideals but make their principles and ideals subserve their inclinations to enable them to act as they desire.[61] Or, as Toynbee likes to put it: "We are betrayed by what is false within." Yes! And even when we are anti-Semites, to look for the cause of our failure outside of ourselves is one of the signs of a spiritual breakdown.

Apparently Toynbee himself is not fully convinced of the validity of his ingenious interpretation of Christian anti-Semitism, which pronounces "the murdered not the murderer" to be guilty. After all, Judaism gave birth not only to Christianity but also to Mohammedanism. "Why was it that the Christians, when they eventually came into political power, distinguished themselves so disadvantageously from their Muslim contemporaries by abusing this power in their behavior towards the Jews?"[62] Mr. Toynbee's answer is that the attacks against Jews and Pharisees which are contained in the New Testament served as a constant stimulus for the breeding of Christian anti-Semitism. Thus, he is enabled to establish a connection between the martyrdom that Jewry suffered at the hand of Christendom through the ages and the crucifixion of Jesus. Of course, he is not just repeating the old threadbare theory from the Dark and Middle Ages—to this day not completely without potency in certain parts of Christendom—that the Jews have been punished for the crime of "deicide," committed by their remote ancestors. After all, Mr. Toynbee is a modern historian. Although he still clings to everyone of the old prejudices and superstitions concerning the Jews and Judaism, he does make an effort to equip them with a semblance of rationality.[63] In keeping with the persistent Christian belief since the early days of the Church, Toynbee sees in the Martyrdom of Jewry through the centuries the "deadly recoil on Jewish heads of the shedding of Jesus' blood." But, being an enlightened historian, he does not trouble God to execute the punishment; instead he explains it as the natural result of the effect of the Jewish attitude to Jesus, as presented in the New Testament, on Christian souls. He comes to the cynical conclusion that, "in gently submitting to be put to death . . . Jesus had involuntarily done his own people immeasurably greater harm than they had subsequently suffered at Muhamad's Gentile hands. . . ."[64] However, one is unable to accept the notion that a being which according to Toynbee is the incarnation of God Himself and identical with Him could ever have done anything "involuntarily." In 1954 the English historian echoes the words of the rabidly anti-Semitic Greek Father of the Church, John Chrysostom, who more than fifteen hundred years earlier wrote: "The Jews have assasinated the Son of God! . . . you dare to associate with this nation of assassins and hangmen! . . . O Jewish people! A man crucified by your hands has been stronger than you and has destroyed you and scattered you. . . ."[65] There are indeed times when even a Jew might be tempted to agree with the Toynbean dictum that human nature is so constituted that moral and spiritual progress is unachievable in history.[66]

However, it might have been possible to make some contribution toward a better understanding of the issue of progress had Toynbee's eagerness for historic justice not been satisfied merely by noticing "the recoil of the shedding of Jesus' blood" on the heads of so many generations of Jews, who—whatever the historic truth of the crucifixion—were free from even the slightest suspicion of personal guilt. Discussing the various forms of man's inhumanity to man, our author has written a fine chapter under the title "Dehumanization." There he makes a very relevant statement—and again unwittingly in the best of Pharisaic tradition—about the nemesis that follows from treating a human being who happens to be at our mercy as an "underdog." One fully agrees with Toynbee that the "result achieved by a human being who seeks to rob his fellows of their humanity is to divest himself of his own. . . ."[67] This is what happens to the persecutor, whether he persecutes for religious, cultural, politico-economical, or racial reasons. One shudders to think of the moral consequences of "the recoil" of the shedding of Jewish blood through more than sixteen centuries of triumphant Christianity in the West. The disabilities, the persecutions, the pogroms, the expulsions, the murder, the rape, the plunder, the hatred, and the contempt to which Jewry has been exposed in Christian Europe have their counterpart in the equivalent measure of moral and spiritual contamination that recoiled on the soul of the West from this debauchery of sadism and inhumanity. The endless Western Martyrdom of Israel is also the frightening history of Western "Dehumanization." The manifold moral and ethical failure of the West, so impressively presented by Toynbee's *Study of History,* is not to be understood without the uninterrupted process of "Dehumanization," which was the corollary to Western anti-Semitism. Anti-Semitism has been the most potent, because the most consistent and most self-righteous, factor working for the demoralization of the West. The "cynical conclusion" of the historian is carried closer to the truth by the melancholy observation that

—if the historian is right—"in gently submitting to be put to death," and thus "involuntarily" having done so much harm "to his own people," Jesus has "involuntarily" done immeasurably greater harm to his own teaching. Anti-Semitism, as a continuous process of "Dehumanization," has hurt the soul of the West no less than the body of Jewry in the West. Thinking of the Martyrdom of Israel in the domain of Western civilization, but not losing sight of the corresponding process of Western "Dehumanization," a Jew may find some comfort in the thought that it is better to suffer wrong than to do it.[68] Or as Isaiah put it—to mention only one among the prophets and teachers of Israel who gave expression to the principle of "Dehumanization"—"Woe unto their soul! For they have wrought evil unto themselves."[69]

IV. TOYNBEE'S OPINIONS ON
JEWISH SURVIVAL

1. THE DIASPORA AS THE FOSSILIZED "SURVIVAL" OF
JUDAISM AND JEWRY

1.

IN THE OPINION of Mr. Toynbee, Jewish history, as well as the history of Judaism, came to an end in 69-70 C.E., when the Roman legions destroyed Jerusalem and the Jewish people were scattered over the face of the earth. The catastrophe, we have seen him maintain, was due to the spiritual failure of Jewry to appreciate the significance of the message of Jesus, which offered the only solution to the problems of the times. As to the Jewry that has survived to this day, the most pleasant thing he can say is that it is "the debris" of a "devoted Syriac people," which existed once upon a time; that it represents nothing more than "a pulverized social ash."[1] In other places, of course, he is more definite and calls the "pulverized social ash" a fossil. What exactly he means by these various appellations is not easy to ascertain. As we have so often had opportunity to observe, eloquent ambiguity and a luxuriant literary inexactitude are the most distinguishing features of the Toynbean style; and so they remain in the case of the "Jewish fossil."

Surveying the various extant civilizations, Toynbee "discerns" Jewry as one of the two sets "of what appear to be fossilized relics of similar societies now extinct." Having once "appeared" to be fossil, soon Jewry becomes "manifestly" a fossil—without any reason being given either for the appearance or for the manifestation.[2] At this early stage of the *Study* one might assume that Toynbee does not mean to convey more than that Jewry does not really *belong* to the West, or to the other dominant civilizations of the East, although it once did belong to a civilization of a category similar to the now "living" ones;

83

there is therefore something "abnormal" about Jewry. He is, however, much more insistent, and still more obscure, in other places. At times, *Jewry* is the fossil; at others, it is *Judaism*. Judaism, again, "is a fossil of the extinct Syriac *Civilization*." But not always: sometimes Judaism is "a fossil of Syriac *religion* as it was before the Hellenic impact. . . ."[3] But a fossilized community is not the same as a fossilized religion; nor is it understandable how Judaism may be, at the same time, a fossil of a civilization as well as that of a religion—especially in view of the fact that one of the important points of the *Study* is the interpretation of the essential difference that exists between a Civilization and a Higher Religion.[4] When an author is so unchaste in his language, one cannot help suspecting that beyond his desire to be negative and censorious he has little to contribute to the understanding of the subject which he pretends to discuss. Let us see what meaning—if any—might be attributed to both the idea of a fossilized Jewry and that of a fossilized Judaism within the context of the Toynbean scheme of history.

What could be meant by fossilized Jewry? How can human beings, who breathe and live and work and hope and aspire, be fossils? Even assuming that Jews, by "resting on their oars" and rejecting Jesus, lost their creativity, are people who are not "creative" not alive? And, as long as there is life, may a faculty once lost never again be regained? Or does creativity and life depend exclusively on faith in Jesus? If so, why does Toynbee not say so? Why does he not state without equivocation, and with the courage of conviction—for which one could respect him, even though one might not agree with him—that all men, Jew or Gentile, are fossils unless they accept Jesus as the "Son of God?" Occasionally he writes with great fervor of the "sacrosanctity of each single soul in the eyes of God."[5] How then can Jews be fossils? Have they no souls? Or does Toynbee here too follow the Church Father, Chrysostom, who taught that every Jew was a temple of the devil and "I would say the same things about their souls"?[6] But even so they would still be alive, and as long as there is life there is hope that the "temple of the devil" might yet be turned into a temple of God.

Toynbee stubbornly refuses to pay any attention either to the part that Jews have played in the history of Western civilization or to the internal life of Jewry in the midst of Western Christendom. Typically, he acknowledges only "the whole-heartedness and virtuosity with which all Jews in the West—Ritualists, Liberals, and Zionists alike—participated in the secular activities of the Western Gentile World on the *economic plane.'*" No mention is made of the rich and significant contribution by Jews to the culture and civilization of all Western nations through the ages. There is no need to list all the outstanding Jews who have creatively participated in the secular activities of the West on the literary, cultural, artistic, scholarly, and political plane. All the nations of the earth have been enriched by their life work.[8] One of Toynbee's greatly admired masters, Henri Bergson, whose ideas are responsible for important sections of the *Study,* was—as is well known—a child of the Jewish people. Spinoza, Heine, Disraeli, Mendelssohn, Meyerbeer, Paul Ehrlich, Rathenau, Stephan Zweig, Freud, Einstein, to mention only a few and at random, were all Jews. Of course, it may be easy to say that these men of genius were Jews only by birth and "Gentiles" by culture. But keeping in mind what modern psychology has taught us about the importance of early impressions and influences on the entire life of a human being, how are the Jewish fathers and mothers, the Jewish home, the Synagogue, the Jewish community, and the Jewish ethos to be separated from the bearers of these great names? Who will dare to say where the Jewish influence ends and the Gentile one begins? What sense does it make to call a community fossilized that counts such men among its children? The Nazis declared them all "bloody Jews," Mr. Toynbee tries to "embezzle" them.

As to the internal life of the Jewish community, it makes still less sense to speak of fossilization. All through the long and dark centuries of the Diaspora there was the Jewish family, the cornerstone of the Jewish community. The ethical standards of Jewish family life have been for many centuries among the highest in the Western world. Toynbee himself cannot but agree that "the loftly conception of family life ... had, of course,

been derived by the Christian Church from a Jewry that has
been its matrix .... This high standard in the sphere of family
relations had been one of the most striking features by which
the social life of the Jews in the diaspora had been distinguished, to its credit, from the contemporary life of a post-
Alexandrine Hellenic Society...."⁹ He would have remained
still within the boundaries of historic truth had he made the
comparison not only with "the post-Alexandrine Hellenic Society" but even with the post-Constantine Christian Society. Con-
cubinage, adultery, and prostitution were hardly known in the
Judengasse; whereas wife-beating was permitted by canon law
in the twelfth and thirteenth centuries, in the rabbinical Re-
sponsa of the time one finds that "this is a thing not done in
Israel." Wife-beating was considered by the Rabbis as sufficient
ground for divorce.

All through the centuries of the Diaspora there existed a
carefully worked-out system of general and public education.
The historian Cecil Roth of Oxford has written of the educational system in the European Diaspora:

> Enrollment for either sex was free. The number of
> pupils in each class was regulated. The elements of the
> vernacular were taught as well as Hebrew. Meals were
> given to those who required them. Boots and clothing were
> distributed to the most needy in winter. A community of
> less than 1000 souls, in the eighteenth-century Italy, would
> maintain a school of this type, with no less than six teach-
> ers and assistants. The scheme of education was not re-
> stricted (as might be imagined) to quasi-theological
> studies, but, by reason of the wide humanity of Judaism,
> necessarily extended to every field of human interest.
> When Germany, for example, had hardly emerged from
> barbarism, there were in the Rhineland Jewish schools,
> to which students streamed from every part of the world,
> hardly distinguishable from the primitive universities
> which Christian Europe was beginning to develop at this
> period . . . in 1466, the handful of Jews living in Sicily
> . . . received formal license from the King to open their

own properly-constituted University, with faculties of Medicine, Law, and presumably the Humanities. Twenty-four years later, the idea was revived in Northern Italy.[11]

No less well developed and highly organized were the charitable and welfare institutions and services of the Jewish Ghetto. These associations took care of the poor in all emergencies from childbirth to burial. To quote again the words of Mr. Roth:

> Every Ghetto had its Lodging House for indigent strangers, which was also used as hospital (the institution is found at Cologne as early as the eleventh century); every community had its salaried physician, so that medical attendance was available for all. There was, too, a free educational system, supported by voluntary subscriptions, and open to every child. . . . As early as the fourth century, the Emperor Julian, when he ordered the institution of inns for strangers in every city, referred with admiration to the example of the Jews, "the enemies of the Gods, in whose midst no beggars were to be found."[12]

Before the barbarous destruction of European Jewry the oldest educational and welfare systems and the longest history of a civilized and humane communal organization in Europe belonged to the Jews. The accomplishment was the greater since it was not supported by any state authority and was inspired and sustained through the centuries, and even at the darkest times of persecution, by the voluntary, self-imposed social, ethical, and religious discipline of the Jewish people. The record of the internal life of Diaspora Jewry seems to suggest a vitality which is impressive—and which bears no likeness to fossilization.

2.

If the term "fossil" is senseless in its application to the living community of the Jews, may it not have validity in connection with Judaism? Here we seem to find firmer ground; Toynbee, for a change, does indicate what he means. After the "transformation" of Judaism by the Maccabees into a political instrument, this higher religion "lost its message for Mankind and has hardened into a 'fossil' of the extinct Syriac society. . . ."[13] Here, at least, a reason is given for the fossilization. However, assuming that the Toynbean interpretation of the Maccabean period is correct, one recalls that the failure of the Maccabees has been repeated and, indeed, surpassed by the four living religions of Toynbee. Islam was "politically debauched" by its founder, and the other Higher Religions experienced the tragedy of "political debauchery" at later stages. Like the other Higher Religions, Christianity was overtaken by the same tragedy when "it incarnated itself in a *Republica Christiana* or when the modern Protestant variation of the same Western Christianity . . . allowed itself to become the established religion of this or that secular parochial successor-state of the abortive ecclesiastical commonwealth of Pope Gregory VII and Pope Innocent II."[14] Nowhere does Toynbee indicate that any of the "Big Four" living religions hardened into a fossil because it was "transformed into a political weapon." Of course, he is quite right; for whatever the sins of even the prophets and the highest ecclesiastics of a religion may be, they will certainly never be visited on the message of that religion. Whatever truth there is in the message, it remains valid, no matter to what use frail human beings may put it. Toynbee is right in refusing to identify the failure of Mohammed with that of Islam or those of Christendom with that of Christianity. He is wrong when he gives up this position of sanity and insists that the Maccabean sins led to the fossilization of Judaism. The vitality of a Higher Religion is of the Spirit; it can never become fossilized. There may always be "ears that do not hear and eyes that do not see." Thus the precepts "Thou shalt love the Lord, thy God . . . ." or "Love thy neighbor as thyself," or "Righteousness, righteousness thou shalt pursue," or "The works of My hands are drowning in the sea and you dare sing My praise," may "lose their message for mankind." But the religious and ethical validity of the message can never be vitiated by human shortcomings.

Toynbee's systematic expropriation of Jewish concepts for the benefit of Christianity, which we have had occasion to observe, is in itself a proof of the vitality of Judaism. Numerous are the cases in the *Study* which show that, even when dealing with the most acute problems of man, the guidance of the Jewish Bible is still indispensable. We have also noted that Toynbee's cherished idea of the "heavenly harmony" in which the four living religions are component parts was "not in Christian terms," whereas it might well have been in Jewish, i.e., Pharisaic, terms. Let two examples illustrate to what extent even an anti-Judaic and anti-Jewish author like Mr. Toynbee is subject to the influence of the Judaic Spirit.

In the ninth volume of the *Study* there is an interesting chapter on the relation of "Law and Freedom in History."[15] The riddle of the relationship between the Law of God as manifest in God's Creation and the freedom of the human soul is recognized as "the most difficult and the most crucial of all questions." Significantly enough, it is only now that Toynbee discovers that God is not only Love but also Power, "as revealed in the Gospels," says he—and, one might add, as known to every half-educated Jewish teenager from the Jewish Bible. Indeed nothing could be more childish than to say, God is Love, and not Power, in the face of the crushing manifestations of His "Power" in the universe. The Toynbean answer to the riddle of human freedom as opposed to the Law of physical nature is that "Love suspends the fiat of Omnipotence in order to transmute a command into a challenge which confronts the human recipient of it with a free choice between Good and Evil and between Life and Death."[16] We doubt that Toynbee has succeeded in solving the problem of free will and rather think that not much sense may be associated with the suspension of the fiat of Omnipotence by Love. However, the idea that man stands before the choice between Life and Death, equipped by God with the freedom, and therefore also with the responsibility, to choose Life, not only is based on a famous text from the Jewish Bible[17] but has been fundamental in Judaism from the beginning of Jewish history to this day. On the other hand, while Toynbee's description of the choice as a spiritual struggle "between an aspiration towards Grace and a gravitation towards Original Sin" is couched in Christian terminology, the very idea of man's freedom to choose between

Good and Evil was rejected by outstanding representatives and schools of Christian tradition and theology. It is not easily reconciled with the words of the Christian apostle Paul: "The good that I would I do not: but the evil which I would not, that I do."[18] As is well known, the Pauline standpoint became the basis of the theories of predestination espoused by such later Christians as Augustine and Calvin. For Luther too, the very idea of Original Sin excluded the possibility of free will. According to a rich vein in Christian tradition, salvation can never be deserved by man; it is a pure act of Grace on the part of God, and no one can say why some are saved and others damned. It is true that, especially in Catholicism, salvation depends on works as well as on faith; yet in all Christianity— as became apparent in the Pelagian controversy—free will has found rather uncomfortable accommodation side by side with Original Sin. Whenever it is maintained "that human freedom springs from an encounter in which Man is summoned to respond to a challenge presented by God," people are attempting to solve their problems in terms of basic Judaism.

The other illustration of Judaism's undiminished vitality, as demonstrated by Mr. Toynbee's own "Jewishness," one recognizes in connection with the Toynbean concept of Transfiguration.[19] Again we are inclined to believe that Toynbee himself is not quite sure what he means by the mystery of Transfiguration. It is a kind of overcoming of this world and, when it happens, the most important event in the life of a man. Whatever it may be, there is a "reckoning of spiritual values" which corresponds to it and which remains unknown without it. The basic principle of this "transfigured" reckoning of values was revealed by Jesus, when he said: "For what shall it profit a man, if he shall gain the whole world, and lose his own soul?" The new reckoning of values was, nevertheless, anticipated by "the first and greatest and most Christian of all the Hellenic philosophers," Plato, from whose various writings one may compose this quotation: ". . . we must not allow ourselves to be carried away by anything in the World—not by honors, not by riches, not by power, and not by poetry either. For none of these things is worth the price of neglecting Righteousness and the rest of what constitute Virtue."[20] Actually, there was no need to compose a Platonic quotation from various separate passages of the philosopher. This same "reckoning of spiritual values" was given expression in much more powerful and passionate language, almost three centuries before Plato and more than six centuries before Jesus, by the Jewish prophet Jeremiah, when he proclaimed:

Thus saith the Lord:
Let not the wise man glory in his wisdom,
Neither let the mighty man glory in his might,
Let not the rich man glory in his riches:
But let him that glorieth glory in this,
That he understandeth and knoweth me,
That I am the Lord which exercise mercy,
Justice, and righteousness, in the earth:
For in these things I delight,
Saith the Lord.[21]

The Jewish prophet is much more specific than Plato and goes far beyond him; nor has anyone since the days of Jeremiah improved on this ranking of values. The Pharisaic tradition in the Midrash has rightly recognized in this passage the most conclusive summary of the highest good in Judaism; and the great Jewish philosopher of the Middle Ages, who was also one of the greatest codifiers of the Law, Moses Maimonides, found the ultimate issue of his entire philosophical system expressed in these words of the prophet.[22] In his "reckoning of spiritual values" Toynbee only proves the potency of Judaism, even though he may be too ungenerous to acknowledge his indebtedness to it. In contrast to Toynbee, the Nazis recognized that the spirit of Judaism, far from being fossilized, was all-pervading; there was no escaping it, without throwing overboard the Jewish "reckoning of spiritual values."

2. ZIONISM—OR THE FOSSIL AS THE ARCH-CRIMINAL OF HISTORY

1.

Whatever the exact meaning of the fossil theory may be,

there is no doubt in the mind of Mr. Toynbee as to the proper significance of Diaspora Jewry. It alone is the "historic Jewry," and the "essence of Jewishness" is a masterly adaptation to a Diaspora environment, which is achieved by "a meticulous devotion to the Mosaic Law"—a rather inferior code—"and a consummate virtuosity in commerce and finance."[23] Jewry has been embedded as "a fossil of alien origin . . . in the body of Western Christendom since its pre-natal days"; it does not belong to the West and it is not part of it. It does not really belong anywhere, and therefore it is "at home" only in the isolation of the Czarist "Pale" or the Ghetto. Final and irrevocable disappearance of Jewry through assimilation might have been the best that could have happened to it. Unfortunately, this was prevented by Zionism, which adopted an archaistic imitation of the idol of Western nationalism.[24] Worst of all, by its establishment of the state of Israel, Zionism has even been successful. From the standpoint of the Toynbean philosophy of history, the Diaspora is a bothersome nuisance; but a Zionism that has actually led to the re-emergence of ancient Judea as a modern state drives Toynbee to exasperation. The annals of human history are, unfortunately, crowded with the most sordid crimes imaginable; yet Mr. Toynbee's righteous indignation is nowhere as intense as in his unqualified condemnation of the Zionists. According to him, the Zionists, acting on "the principle of making the defenseless pay," on the 14th of May, 1948, set up "a state of Israel in Palestine by force of arms in a war that had resulted in more than half a million Palestinian Arabs losing their homes, in compensation for atrocities committed against Jews in . . . 1933-1945, not in the Levant, but in Europe, and not by Arabs, but by Germans." It was because of "the sympathy of the Western World with the Jews over their sufferings at Germany's hands" that the Zionists were able to obtain "a retrospective condonation from the UNO for their violation of the rights of the Arab people of Palestine."[25]

The truth is that in 1948 Zionism had already been in existence for more than fifty years, and therefore its aspiration could not have been to seek compensation for the German atrocities of 1933-1945. The Jewish state came into being because it had been in the process of being built for more than half a century, with an unprecedented heroism of peaceful colonizing and with Jewish sweat, Jewish blood, and Jewish tears. Zionism sought the answer to the problem of the "fossil" that, as Toynbee so eloquently proves, belonged nowhere; it strove to put an end to many centuries of Jewish martyrdom, suffered not only at German hands but at the hands of both Christendom and Islam. The Jewish state was *established* not by force of arms but by the will of the highest international authority ever known in history, by the U.N. decision on the partition of Palestine of November 29, 1947 (which is not even mentioned in the *Study*); it was *defended* by the force of arms. The "Zionists" were the men and women of the Yishuv, together with their children and old people, surrounded by half a dozen independent Arab states. Seven Arab armies, among them the British-trained, British-equipped, and British-officered Arab Legion, were preparing for the invasion of Palestine. The "Zionists" staked their entire existence, their own lives and those of their wives and children, in a conflict which was forced upon them and in which all the odds were against them. It was indeed a miracle of faith and heroism that the Arab armies were defeated in their publicly avowed intention of repeating the Hitlerite German massacres on Palestinian Jewry. The statement that, in establishing the Jewish state, the Zionists acted on "the principle of making the defenceless pay" is among the meanest and most despicable pronouncements that have ever issued from the pen of a historian.

It is, however, not our intention to line up all the facts in order to disprove Mr. Toynbee. They cannot be unknown to him. There was a time when he wrote with sanity about Zionism. In the second volume of the *Study* he recognized that in the Eastern European countries assimilation was not possible, and that even in Western Europe it was "an essential part of the Jew's identity" that he was "a member of the living Jewish community and an heir to the ancient Jewish tradition." He realized that Zionism was opposed to assimilationism because the Jew "cannot cut off his Jewishness and cast it from him without self-mutilation . . ."; its ultimate aim was "to liberate the Jewish people from the peculiar psychological complex induced by the penalization to which they have been subject for centuries in the Gentile World." About Nazism he wrote that "it still further strengthened the already strong Zionist case. . . ." The social philosophy of the Zionist movement he thought "has already been justified by results." While he appreciated even in that earlier volume that there was a tragic element in the inability of the Zionists to reach an understanding with the Arabs, he was still fair enough to concede that, as always, two parties were needed to reach an understanding. At that stage of the *Study* Toynbee still acknowledged that "the very spirit of Western Nationalism which has been the inspiration of Zionism itself" had captured the Arabs too and roused them to resistance.[26]

2.

Mr. Toynbee's change of attitude toward Zionism might be, in itself, a matter of small significance. It does, however, require closer scrutiny on account of the very fury of his moral indignation. After saying some very moving words about the "lasting infamy of Western Man," as revealed in the Western crime toward the Negroes and in the extermination of the Jewish Diaspora in the European homeland of Western Christendom, Mr. Toynbee proceeds to the unveiling of the most original discovery of his entire *Study*—the one for which he will be remembered long after his extensive writings will have fallen into oblivion. Indeed, it required a genius of a sort to see, as clearly as Toynbee does, that "the Nazi Gentile's fall was less tragic than the Zionist Jews'." This is how the statement is justified:

On the morrow of a persecution in Europe in which they had been the victims of the worst atrocities ever known to have been suffered by Jews or indeed by any other human beings, the Jews' immediate reaction to their own experience was to become persecutors in their turn for the first time since . . . 135 [c.e.]—and this at the first opportunity that had since arisen for them to inflict on other

94

human beings who had done the Jews no injury. . . .
In . . . 1948 some 684,000 out of some 859,000 Arab
inhabitants of the territory of Palestine which the Zionist
Jews conquered by force of arms in that year lost their
homes and property and became destitute "displaced
persons."[27]

It is a well-known streak in the Gentile mentality to inflate any
wrong done by the Jews and to minimize the wrong done to
them. The reference to the year 135 c.e., the previous occasion
when Jews were persecutors, is a psychologically revealing slip
of memory. The date is that of the collapse of the Bar Kokba
rebellion against Rome. In the mind of Mr. Toynbee, an act of
rebellion against oppression by a foreign invader, when it is
undertaken by Jews, becomes associated with persecution.
Those wicked Jews were persecuting the poor defenseless Roman Empire, which had done them no injury. To quote one
of Mr. Toynbee's own quotations:

Cet animal est tres méchant:
Quand on l'attaque, il se defend.[28]

While this natural propensity of the Gentile mentality is un-
mistakably present in Toynbee, it does not suffice to explain his
inexhaustible originality. Not only are the Zionists worse than
the Nazis, but they are actually the arch-criminals of all history.
Says Toynbee:

If the heinousness of sin is to be measured by the degree
to which the sinner is sinning against the light that God
has vouchsafed to him, the Jews had even less excuse in
. . . 1948 for evicting Palestinian Arabs from their homes
than Nebuchadnezzar and Titus and Hadrian and the
Spanish and Portuguese Inquisition had had for uproot-
ing, persecuting, and exterminating Jews in Palestine and
elsewhere at divers times in the past. In . . . 1948 the Jews
knew, from personal experience, what they were doing;
and it was their supreme tragedy that the lesson learnt by
them from their encounter with the Nazi German Gentiles should have been not to eschew but to imitate some

of the evil deeds that the Nazis had committed against the Jews.[29]

When it comes to the moral evaluation of a deed, and its comparison with other deeds in the same category, all discussion comes to a standstill. Value judgments are subjective affirmations, which can be neither proved nor disproved. From the point of view of a person who does not accept Toynbee's evaluation, his sweeping condemnation of the Zionist Jews is tantamount to a "debauchery" of righteous indignation. Since, however, in so far as it has any relation to the world of facts, the Toynbean judgment is based on the Toynbean premise that the Jews set up a state in Palestine by force of arms, that the immediate reaction to their own experience was "to become persecutors in their turn," that they acted on "the principle of making the defenseless pay," it is obvious that Mr. Toynbee badly needs his righteous indignation. No one makes such fanatically wild accusations against others without some inner compulsion. Mr. Toynbee clings to his distortions and to his indignation against the "Zionists" for the sake of his own peace of mind.

V. UNDERSTANDING TOYNBEE

WHEN A MAN makes himself guilty of so many distortions of fact, when he judges with such pretense to authority on the basis of such bottomless ignorance of the subject, when he levels such unbridled accusations against another religion and another people, as does Toynbee in his treatment of Judaism and Jewry, it is not enough to show up his ignorance, his mistakes and misrepresentations. One must also attempt to answer the question: Why does he do it?

Toynbee's picture of Judaism and Jewry has very little to do with either of them; it is determined mainly by his attitude toward some of the basic issues of human existence in general and his evaluation of Christianity in particular.

1. TOYNBEE'S NEED FOR A MUNDANE JEWISH MESSIANISM

The writing of the *Study* must have taken its author a considerable number of years. The impact of the material and moral catastrophes that have shaken our world since the early 1930's is felt in most of the pages of the latter parts of Toynbee's work. Many of the great issues of all history became acute problems of the day while Toynbee was writing. As he wrote, so he struggled with his philosophy of history—often changing his views and all the time himself changing. There are at least two Toynbees in the ten volumes. The break is most obvious between Volumes V and VI.

The violently negative tone toward Judaism, which dominates the sixth volume and compares so unfavorably with what is said previously and even contradicts it, is a symptom of the change that must have occurred in Toynbee himself. One may recognize it in the vital variation in the interpretation of the, by now, familiar concept of Transfiguration. As we have seen, Transfiguration is a focal point in the entire Toynbean philosophy. It is the only solution to the problem of the breakdown and disintegration of a civilization and society. In Volume V,

97

Transfiguration is "a change in spiritual climate" which is brought about by "a form of transference of the field of action from the Macrocosm to the Microcosm," which is identical with "the criterion of the growth of a civilization."[1] According to this definition, Transfiguration is a task for man to undertake and fulfill. In Volume VI, however, Toynbee reaches the conclusion that Transfiguration is the perceiving of the Kingdom of God, effected by the operation of the Spirit; transfiguring the world, the Spirit redeems it. At the same time, Transfiguration is a mystery that is beyond our understanding; it is a mystery because it is an act of God and an effect of God's presence.[2] Whatever may be the meaning of all this, it is obvious that Transfiguration is not a task that can be performed by man. Man cannot save or redeem himself; "salvation belongeth unto the Lord" alone. Unless the would-be savior of mankind is "in some sense divine" he will be impotent to execute his mission. Therein lies the significance of the Christian doctrine that Jesus is identical with the Godhead.

It appears that with Toynbee this is not just theology or dogmatic faith; it is the conclusion he reaches from his study of history. He is a historian disillusioned with man and civilization. The crimes, the failures, the beastly inhumanity that crowd the annals of man's history, prove to Toynbee that human nature is basically perverse. Therefore whatever man may undertake in order to save himself always fails. Liberalism's idol is Homunculus; that of Communism, Leviathan. "Democracy" is "this disinterred Attic blessed word"; it and Industrialism constitute the twin demons of the West; it only pays lip service to Humanitarianism. Western parliaments are "these parliamentary corporate despots." Civilization is no permanent transfiguration of the essence of human nature, but merely a brittle "cake of custom"; nor is progress possible. History has been, thus far, mainly "the abominable Age of Civilization, Human Sacrifice, Slavery, and War." Man can do nothing well, and all his hope is in salvation from God.[3] And thus *A Study of History* from the sixth volume onward ceases to be what the title indicates and becomes "History as a Study in Salvation." Mr. Toynbee acknowledges this change of course by saying:

". . . our study has carried us to a point at which the civilizations in their turn, like the parochial states of the Modern Western World at the outset of our investigation, have ceased to constitute intelligible fields of study for us and have forfeited their historical significance except insofar as they minister to the progress of Religion. . . ."[4]

No one may sympathize with Mr. Toynbee over his disillusionment with the human race more sincerely than the Jew; what for Mr. Toynbee is a study of history the Jews have witnessed and suffered and endured in their own lives through the ages. Yet no one will appreciate better than the Jew the irony that a man possessed of such disillusionment and pessimism concerning human nature should turn on Judaism and Jewry. The deeper the disappointment and the more sincere the sorrow of such a man, the more will he resent and reject almost everything Judaism and the Jew stand for in history. The authentic Jew knows failure, his own as well as that of the rest of mankind; he has seldom had opportunity to be much impressed with man, but he never despairs of him. Because the Jew believes in God, he cannot but—in spite of all history— through God believe in man too.

Toynbee is a religious man, but his religion is motivated by despair. His theology of disillusionment compels him to recognize only a mundane Judaism. If it is assumed that Transfiguration is within the grasp of man and is reflected in the ethos of gentleness, the Maccabean and Zealot militancy may be seen as a *departure* from the higher Judaism of a previous period. But once Transfiguration becomes the mystical "renting of the veil" in the Temple, effected by God and revealing His Presence and His Kingdom, it is obvious that prior to that miraculous epiphany the True God could not have been known. It is this position that leads Toynbee to create what we have termed his "psychological" version of Judaism. The act of Transfiguration was the epiphany of Christianity; *ergo*, the Judaism preceding it could have been only a tribal religion with a provincial deity at its center. Since there can be no other Savior than the God Incarnate, Messianism prior to Jesus must have been pure mundane militancy for the sake of a national kingdom and world dominion. All that Judaism could accomplish was to stumble by way of Futurism to the very threshold of Transfiguration.[5]

2. TOYNBEE'S NEED FOR THE "FOSSIL"

1.

Not only does Judaism not fit into the Toynbean scheme of salvation; but also Jewry continually impedes the neatly mapped-out course of Toynbean history. Were it not for Jewry, Mr. Toynbee's "laws" would look much more convincing.

One of these laws of Toynbean history asserts that at the breakdown and disintegration of a civilization the movement of history is carried on by three creative acts: the dominant minority creates the universal state; the internal proletariat, taking over a higher religion which is already a going concern, establishes a universal church; the external proletariat of the barbarians, beyond the confines of the collapsing civilization, enters upon a heroic age.[6] The Jewish people, according to Toynbee's classification, formed one section of the internal proletariat of the Hellenic civilization. The "dominant minority" of Hellenism responded to the challenge of disintegration according to the rule and attempted to bring peace to a sorely tried ecumene by establishing the "Hellenic" universal state, the Roman Empire; at least one part of the "Syriac" internal proletariat was equally obliging and duly responded to the challenge by producing its universal religion, Christianity. Only Jewry had to be different: neither did it establish a Syriac universal state to unify the Syriac world, as was done later by Islam—a task which perhaps it was not its responsibility to undertake—nor did it bring about a universal church, as was done by some Syriac "natives."[7] What ails Toynbee is revealed in the earlier part of the *Study,* when his anti-Jewish and anti-Judaic attitude has not yet crystallized and he is not yet fully aware how seriously his "laws" are disrupted by Jewish behavior. About the survival of Jewry he writes: "The ancient Syriac neighbours of Israel have fallen into the melting-pot and have been re-minted, in the fullness of time with new images and superscriptions, while Israel has proved impervious to this alchemy—performed by History in the crucibles of *universal states* and *universal churches* and *wanderings of the nations*—to which the Gentiles all in turn succumb."[8] Jewry did neither of the things that a people is supposed to do at a time of crisis—and yet it has survived. In the form of Futuristic militancy it gave an altogether wrong answer to the challenge; it ran afoul of the "laws" of history; its survival is therefore inexplicable in terms of those laws. What is therefore to be done with Jewry? How is it to be classified? With disarming frankness, at this earlier phase of the *Study,* Toynbee explains in a footnote to the passage we have just quoted that "from the Gentile standpoint" modern Jewry is the fossil remnant of a society which is now extinct. This does make sense. All it says is that from the Gentile—or, perhaps more correctly, from the Toynbean—standpoint the survival of Jewry cannot be explained. Jewry *ought* to have disappeared therefore it *has* disappeared; its continued existence must be a state of fossilization.

However, as the main theme of the *Study* develops, the problem posed for the entire philosophy of Toynbee becomes more and more serious. One might, perhaps, allow an exception to the "laws" of history, but Jewry's survival is contrary to the "Law" of salvation. For not only is the creation of a universal church by the internal proletariat a better response than any other, but it is the only response that may save man. The peace of the universal state is only transitory. The universal state, as well as the barbarian heroic ages, must perish. There is no salvation for man apart from placing his treasure "in the spiritual exercise of propagating a higher religion." The higher religion that Jewry should have embraced and propagated was Christianity; instead—according to Toynbee—the Jews took the sword. But he who takes the sword *must* perish by the sword; it is the law that brings empires low and eliminates the barbarian war-bands.[9] The "laws" of history are the Will of God; there can be no exception to them. And so the subjectivity of the earlier position is dropped, and Jewry becomes a fossil not only from the Gentile standpoint but in the absolute sense of the word, a fossil in the sight of the Lord Himself. Nevertheless, it still amounts to nothing more than that Jewish survival baffles Toynbee. It is contrary to his scheme of salvation, which has become identical with history. Jewry cannot be alive; its life must be a death-life, a form of life in death, an existing non-existence, a fossil.[10]

2.

Unfortunately, Mr. Toynbee's worries are not yet at an end. Even in the eyes of its creator, the "fossil" theory has still to be propped up. Jewry must be a fossil because it perished at the time of the so-well-deserved destruction of Jerusalem. All right! But fossils are preserved either in certain geological strata, which happen to offer protection for them, or in natural-history museums, which do the same, taking good care of their fossils with the help of expert knowledge dedicated to their preservation. In natural history there are no fossils that have "survived" centuries of assault, carried out with the utmost ruthlessness and with every possible means of destruction. Yet, if Jewry is a fossil, it is exactly this kind of a fossil that it must be. Rather than solving the problem, the "fossil" theory exacerbates it. If Jewry, having had no more vitality to live, had to die, how could it possess the inexhaustible energy needed to "survive" the long and dark centuries of inhumanity and barbarity? In such circumstances the "survival" of a fossil is even more mysterious than that of an active living organism.

Mr. Toynbee is not unaware of this problem. He is obviously deeply impressed by the phenomenon of Jewish survival, as shown by his numerous references to it. He even attempts to find an explanation for it. The fossil remnant of the extinct Syriac civilization was able to "survive" because after the fall of Jerusalem, it was endowed by Rabbi Johanan ben Zakkai "with an inertly rigid institutional framework and a passively obstinate psychological habitus that enabled it to preserve its distinctive communal life in the frail clay tenement of a politically impotent diaspora." What is meant by the "inertly rigid institutional framework" and the "passively obstinate psychological habitus" is made sufficiently clear in other places. It is "the meticulous observance of the Mosaic Law by orthodox Jews who had faithfully followed Rabbi Johanan ben Zakkai's admonitions to seek in the practice of this social drill their palladium for preserving their distinctive communal identity in diaspora."[11] One may be somewhat surprised to hear that inertia, rigidity, passivity, and obstinacy are conducive to survival. Survival depends on adaptability to environment or ability to change one's environment; in either case, what is needed is elasticity, alertness, and creativity.

Mr. Toynbee does say a great deal of blatant nonsense, especially as regards Judaism and Jewry—but not without reason. Not only must he explain the "survival" of the fossil in circumstances in which fossils never survive, but he must be careful not to permit the fossil any measure of sensitivity. A "sensitive fossil" not only would be a contradiction in terms but would still further derange the Toynbean scheme and "laws" of history. The breakdowns of civilizations are the birth-pangs of the Higher Religions. Toynbee cannot repeat often enough that suffering is the key to salvation; it is in human suffering that God reveals himself to man.[12] But here is a people that has known more suffering than any other branch of the human family, that has been crucified for many centuries, generation after generation. Not enough that Jewry hs survived, it has also "drained the cup of staggering" and thus, perchance, it may even hold the key to salvation. Toynbee begrudges Jewry nothing more than its survival and its martyrdom. This people, that should have perished for taking the sword, is the only one in the entire realm of Christendom that for nineteen centuries lived without the sword and survived in the Jesus-like manner, by submitting to abuse, insult, and slaughter. It must never be! And so Toynbee proceeds to rob Jewry not only of life but also of sensitivity. According to Toynbee the nineteen centuries of Jewish Diaspora were "living without disaster." The descendants of the Jewish Quietists for sixty generations rendered themselves successfully "insensible to the painfulness of the mundane Present by a minute observance of a God-given law and by a patient expectation of a Kingdom which is to be established on Earth in God's own time by God's omnipotence alone, without the lifting of one human finger."[13] The "social-drill" Judaism is the very obvious explanation of the survival of the Jewish fossil; it equipped Jewry with all the power and strength that are consistent with the condition of being dead: with inertia, rigidity, obstinacy, passivity, and insensitivity. No wonder it survived! A Jew has no senses, affections, passions. No, he is not fed with the same food, hurt with the same weapons, subject to the same diseases, healed by the same means, warmed and cooled by the same winter and summer, as a Christian is. If you prick him he does not bleed; if you tickle him he does not laugh; if you poison him he does not die. He is a fossil. At last, Shylock has been given his answer.

3. TOYNBEE'S NEED FOR THE ZIONIST ARCH-CRIMINAL

1.

Messianism is of the essence of Judaism and until the rise of Jewish emancipation, chiefly in the 19th century, it was inseparable from the return to Zion. It is therefore rather surprising to find Toynbee insist that Messianism was "finally extinguished" in the defeat of Bar Kokba in 135 C.E. True, our author explains in a footnote: "The word 'finally' holds good, notwithstanding the recent rise of Zionism; for Zionism is a nemesis of the contemporary Nationalism of the Western World and is not a revival of Jewish Futurism which was extinguished at last in the blood of the followers of Bar Kokaba...."[14] One is impressed by a man who has given so many proofs of his ignorance of Judaism, who yet has the audacity to judge what is and is not Jewish. Great and saintly Jews were Zionists, but Toynbee "knows" that the only Jewish attitude is that of the Quietist Agudath Israel, which leaves the return to Zion entirely to God. Actually, as far back as the third century C.E. we find among the leading teachers of the Talmudic era representatives of both the activist and the quietist schools of thought; there were those who considered it a religious duty to leave Babylon and to settle in the Holy Land, as there were others who believed that one had to await the coming of the Messiah in exile. The great codifiers of the Law listed the injunction to live in Erets Israel as one of the 613 commandments of the Torah.[15] But assuming that Zionism is altogether a secular movement and contrary to the Will of God, would it not have been logical to associate it with similar mundane movements in the history of Jewry? Especially, if it is indeed—as Toynbee pretends to believe—nothing but militancy, could it not be a new outburst of the old Maccabean and Zealot ethos of violence? How can he be so sure that Jewish Futurism was finally extinguished in the blood of the followers of Bar Kokba? Might it not have been latent all the time, waiting for the first opportunity to come out into the open?

Presently one realizes that one is once again faced with an assertion that has no basis in history and issues only from Toynbee himself. It is so because it has to be so, by order of the magician Toynbee, whose fertile imagination is tireless in prescribing for history the course it ought to follow. The authentic Jew has always taken the continuity of Judaism and of Jewish history for granted; Toynbee, however, maintains that there is no continuity, for there is no history. How, indeed, could a fossil have history? There is no possibility in Jewry for a renaissance of anything, not even of the mistake of Jewish Futurism. There can be no kind of revival for a fossil. It is interesting to note that the only exile of Jewry which Toynbee recognizes is the Babylonian one. Whereas Judaism and Jewry have for centuries spoken of the Galut, Toynbee speaks only of Diaspora. Exile implies continuity, a past and a future; a Diaspora may have memories of the past, but it has nothing to look forward to. It is for this reason that the historic Jewry is the Diaspora; and the essence of Jewishness, a masterly adaptation to it. According to the requirements of the Toynbean system the other Jewry died when the Diaspora began. Because there can be no return to the past, the Jew is *at home* in the Pale and the Ghetto—and is therefore uprooted when, urged on by Zionism, he moves to Erets Israel. All this, of course, flies in the face of everything that Judaism has ever taught and Jewry ever believed and lived for. It worries Toynbee not a bit. He must distort the facts in order to meet the requirements of his premises.

2.

Toynbee's approach to Zionism is *a priori* negative. For him Zionism is what it has to be, if Mr. Toynbee is to be permitted to continue to cling to his fossil theory of Jewry. He cannot acknowledge the historic connection between the Jewish people and Erets Israel; a fossil has no historic connections that may be translated into a claim or a right. There can therefore be no *return* of the Jews to an ancient homeland. What the Zionists call return is nothing but robbery and, as far as the West is concerned, a compensation granted for Jewish suffering at the expense of the Arabs, who have done the Jews no wrong. But we have still to find the cause of the Toynbean fury against Zionism. For instance, one may understand Toynbee's description of Zionism as a rejection of the historic religion of Israel, even though one may not agree with it. But what is it that motivates him to make the preposterous allegation that the Zionists base the Jewish people's title to Erets Israel "on the physical ground that they were a master race in virtue of 'having Abraham for their father'"; that they caught the "psychic infection from their Nazi persecutors" in ascribing "a rigidly racial significance to the historic distinction between the 'seed of Abraham' and 'the Goyim'"?[16] There is nothing anywhere in Zionist literature or in Zionist policy to lend the slightest justification to such a statement. On the contrary, mundane Zionism sees no virtue whatever in having had "Abraham for their father." It has been its declared objective from the beginning to "normalize" the Jewish people by abolishing the historic distinction between "the seed of Abraham" and "the Goyim," which is usually associated with the religious concept of the covenant between God and Israel. Even if we granted the premise that Zionism was nothing but an imitation of Western nationalism, is all Western nationalism identical with the master-race theory?

The outstanding feature of Toynbee's condemnation of Zionism is the obsessive need to equate Zionism with Nazism and to declare it even more abominable than Nazism. But even he cannot accomplish such a feat on the mundane plane of history. He compares "the fall" of the Gentiles with that of the Zionist Jews. The Zionist crime is so much more heinous because it has to be measured "by the degree to which the sinner is sinning against the light that God has vouchsafed to him"; it is for this reason that the Zionists are worse than Nebuchadnezzar, Titus, and Hadrian, worse even than the Spanish and Portuguese Inquisition. "On the day of Judgment the gravest crime standing to the German National Socialists' account might be, not that they had exterminated a majority of the Western Jews, but that they had caused the surviving remnant of Jewry to stumble."[17] All this is, of course, very nobly said; yet it has no meaning in the context of the political history of the nations. Toynbee, having reached the conclusion that history is meaningless except as a struggle for the salvation of the soul, judges Zionism by the standards of the Kingdom of God. He feels confident he knows what those standards are, even though it is unlikely that they should be revealed to most of mankind before the Day of Judgment. The idea of applying the standards of "The Kingdom" to the evaluation of human behavior is not really new for a Jew. The Pharisees themselves taught that God judges much more strictly the failures of the righteous than those of the unrighteous, for exactly the same reason that Toynbee himself mentions: He judges a man according to the light which He has vouchsafed to him; "He's exacting with the righteous up to a hairbreadth."[18] However, the Pharisees—not so confident as Toynbee that they were sufficiently familiar with the standards of "The Kingdom"— left this kind of superior, Day-of-Judgment judging to God. Bearing in mind their own deficiency, when it came to judging people they taught: ". . . trust not in thyself until the day of thy death; judge not thy neighbour until thou art come into his place."[19] Toynbee, of course, enjoys the great advantage over the Pharisees that "the historian's inspiration" prepared him for the experience of "the Beatific Vision," in which God is seen face to face, "and no longer through a glass darkly."[20] This might well account for the difference.

3.

It is abundantly clear that the association in Toynbee's mind between Zionism and Nazism is not to be separated from his theology of salvation. We shall therefore consider what Zionism and Nazism represent within the scheme of Toynbean salvation.

It was not easy to explain away the continued existence of a people that was supposed to have perished; it was still more difficult to explain the survival of a fossil against which the most fiendish powers of destruction have been arrayed for many centuries. It is exasperating to see the fossil creep back into history. Worst of all, not only do these Jews assert that they are alive, but they maintain that they *return* to their ancient homeland. The return to Zion is affirmed as the continuity of Jewish history and as a chapter in the realization of Jewish Messianism. The Jewish state was established at the end of a period of unparalleled Jewish suffering. If it is the successful response to the challenge of the breakdown and disintegration of Diaspora Jewry, then it is an act of salvation. The Zionist redemption, however, is of the type which Toynbee considers not only insufficient but impossible. Zionism is of "this World" and salvation requires the passing of "this World"; Zionism is effective through the instrumentality of man, but salvation is of God alone. If Zionism is successful, if it is indeed what Jews believe it to be, then Toynbee's "laws" of history and his concept of salvation are invalid. If Israel's return to Zion is redemption, one would have to say of the ten volumes of *A Study of History*: Commit them then to the flames: for they can contain nothing but sophistry and illusion.[21]

This, however, is only one part of the Toynbean dilemma; the Jewish suffering, which was the main impetus in the last phase of Zionist achievement, leads us to the other part: Nazism. What does Nazism stand for in history, understood as man's struggle for salvation? The historian Toynbee does not allow himself the luxury of putting all the blame for the abominable crimes of the concentration camps and crematoria at the door of the Germans alone. Germany is part of the West; it is bone of its bone and flesh of its flesh. Since Germany is surely guilty, so must the non-German Westerner also be.

A Western nation, which for good or evil, had played so central a part in Western history, since the first emergence of a nascent Western Civilization out of a post-Hellenic interregnum, could hardly have committed these flagrant crimes if the same criminality had not been festering foully below the surface of life in the Western World's non-German provinces. The twentieth-century German psyche was like one of those convex mirrors in which a gazer learns to read the character printed on his own countenance through seeing the salient features exaggerated in a revealing caricature. If a twentieth-century Germany was a monster, then, by the same token, a twentieth-century Western Civilization was a Frankenstein guilty of having been the author of this German monster's being.[22]

The guilt of the Germans is the guilt of the West; the fall of Germany, the fall of Western civilization. Toynbee's disillusionment with man sinks to its nadir; the overwhelming Nazi guilt of the West is "a salutary terrifying reminder" of the truth that civilization is "at the mercy of perennial eruptions of Original Sin."[23] The Toynbean theology of despair gains a new and shocking affirmation.

In this manner, Nazism receives an ambivalent significance for the Toynbean philosophy of history: as the overwhelming guilt, reflecting the foully festering criminality of the West, it *confirms* the Toynbean position on the corruptness of human nature and the essential otherworldliness of salvation; as the horrifying martyrdom of the Jewish people, which became the main impetus for the redemption of a shattered Jewry in a successfully re-established Jewish state, it *confounds* everything Toynbee asserts. We have reached a turning point in Toynbean reasoning: these two meanings of suffering imposed by man on man are mutually exclusive. If the suffering *endured* has indeed led to a Jewish-Zionist salvation, then the whole course of history has to be reinterpreted without the Toynbean "laws"; on the other hand, if the suffering *inflicted* is the crime that reveals the truth that man cannot save himself, that man by virtue of Original Sin is by nature a "Nazi," then we are all "Nazis." It is the logical result of the Toynbean philosophy that, since it is impossible to explain history in terms of this-worldly salvation, one must explain it in terms of an other-worldly salvation by Grace. Human suffering inflicted and human suffering endured cannot but prove one and the same thing, namely, that man is bound to fail unless God save him again as He has done once before. Zionism, being an attempt at this-worldly redemption, has to be interpreted, like every-thing else of "this World," as a manifestation of "Nazism." If, as a result of the primordial corruption of human nature, the entire West is "Nazistic," the Jews cannot be an exception. And since suffering is the "key to salvation," the Jewish suffer-ing of the Nazi era, having stirred an ungodly Zionism to even greater activity, has obviously been "misused" for the furtherance of a mundane aim; it therefore only intensifies the Zionist guilt. Mr. Toynbee apparently believes that a few brazen misstatements about Zionist aggression against defense-less Arabs and the mobilization of the standards of the King-dom of God against Zionism may make his thesis sound plausible.

We may now also be able to understand the fury of the Toynbean righteousness. The intellectual requirements of the system are a thousandfold underscored by the emotional needs of the man. Gazing into the "convex mirror" of Nazism and beholding the loathsome caricature of the Western world, he decries—as so often before in the course of history—the gap between the real and the idealized self of the West: the ideal-ized self, as formulated in noble principles of Christianity, and the real self as manifested for Toynbee in the many gruesome failures of Christendom. The higher the ideal, the more dis-gusting its "caricature." But Toynbee has the religious fervor and the moral courage to identify himself with the real as well as the idealized self of the West; thus his loathing of the "caricature" of the West is really a form of "self-contempt." One may observe the sense of hopelessness, which is usually associated with the conflict between a highly idealized and a deeply disappointing self, in the many moving manifestations of Toynbean disillusionment with all civilization and progress. But "self-contempt" is not easily endured, and Toynbee's furiously righteous indignation with Zionism is true to the typical form of escape from it.

When "self-contempt" reaches hardly bearable dimensions one solves the conflict by what psychologists call "externalization," which is a specific form of projection that turns self-loathing into loathing of others. This is how a well-known modern psychologist, Karen Horney, describes the nature of the escape: When self-loathing becomes unbearable, the patient "must fortify himself against it by reinforcing an already existing armor of righteousness. . . . He is compelled, therefore, to externalize his self-contempt, to blame, berate, humiliate others."[24] Blaming, berating, and humiliating Judaism and Jewry are distinctive features of the *Study;* Toynbee's anger against "Zionist" Jews is the badly needed compensation at a moment when, as a result of the Western world's horrifying "Nazistic" failure, the West's self-loathing in him is most intense. The West is bad enough, but it is rather comforting to know that the Jews are even worse. The identification of Zionism with Nazism is accounted for by the well-established pattern of externalization. The rage against oneself is thrust outward and turned against others. It appears "as a specific irritation directed at the very faults in others that the person hates in himself."[25]

As the cases described in Karen Horney's *Our Inner Conflicts* show, it is not at all necessary that the faults for which we berate others should be real; often we impute them to others or exaggerate them in others. "A patient complained of her husband's indecision. Since the indecision concerned a trivial matter, her vehemence was distinctly out of proportion. Knowing her own indecision, I suggested that she had revealed how mercilessly she condemned this in herself." This is a fairly good illustration of the case of Toynbee versus Zionism.

No one denies that the partition of Palestine, as is always true of the partition of any country, was accompanied by a great deal of human suffering and tragic guilt on both sides; but the unbridled vehemence of Toynbee's condemnation of Zionism is out of all proportion to the guilt on the Zionist side. Accusing Zionism of "Nazism" reveals the measure of Toynbee's condemnation of "Nazism" in his own West. The condemnation is so merciless that, in order to render it psychologically bearable for himself, he must project the crime of his West onto others.

The reasons for making Jewry the butt for the externalization of Toynbee's Western "self-loathing" are ample. The "others" in the midst of the Western world—according to the entire structure of the *Study*—are the Jews. The Jews are also constant reminders, and perennial witnesses, to the failure of the West. The Jews have been the challenge for the ethos of gentleness, for the idealized Western self, through the entire history of the West; the unbroken record of Jewish suffering has been the most consistent manifestation of the tragic gap between the real and the idealized self of the Western world— in itself one of the irritating causes of Toynbee's Western "self-loathing." What to do with the silent accusation of Jewish martyrdom? As we saw, Toynbee's rage over the shame of Christian anti-Semitism was at first externalized by making Judaism itself responsible for it; there is no one else in the West to blame for Western failures except oneself or the Jews. The far greater rage over the far more degrading shame of Western "Nazism" is externalized by turning Jewish martyrdom into an accusation against the Jews. Those Zionist Jews, who are "Nazis" just as we of the West are, are really much worse than we ourselves; for, having suffered so badly, they should be much better than we. And with this turn in Toynbee's thinking the pattern of externalization becomes complete to its last detail. "In reality he [the patient] tries to enforce upon the partner the impossible task of realizing his . . . idealized image."[26] Here it is, the perfect projection of Western guilt by means of applying the standards of the "Kingdom of God" to Zionism: if we are "Nazis," at least the Jews, having suffered so much, should have been "Christians!" It is soothing to know that, in spite of all our wickedness, the Jews—the victims of our wickedness—are so much worse than we are. At the same time, the sting of nineteen centuries of Jewish quietism as compared with an equal period of Western aggression has also been eliminated. Jewry was practicing the ethos of gentleness because it had no opportunity to persecute; for witness what the "Nazi-Zionist Sicarii" did to the Arabs, when the first opportunity arose for Jewry to persecute.

To summarize: The Toynbean theology of despair and salvation *impels* Toynbee to explain the Zionist success in terms of the "Nazistic" failure of the West as an affirmation of his disillusionment; the Toynbean Western "self-contempt" *compels* him to a furious and merciless condemnation of "Zionist" Jewry as the only effective means for "externalizing" the Toynbean rage over Western disgrace. To paraphrase Dr. Karen Horney: to strike out against "Zionist" Jewry is for Toynbee a matter of self-preservation.[27]

4. Poor Toynbee!

We shall take one more glance at the net results of Toynbee's struggle for spiritual survival.

The "fossil" survived nineteen centuries of persecution and martyrdom because it was preserved by the "social drill" of the meticulous observance of the Mosaic Law. Or, as he also puts it, Judaism converted itself "into a 'social cement' possessing the astonishing property of being able to hold together a fossilized community in diaspora."[28] Astonishing indeed! We ought to remember that Judaism itself became a fossil following its transformation into a political instrument by the Maccabees. Mr. Toynbee, we must assume, therefore means that a fossilized Judaism converted itself into a "social cement" in order to preserve a fossilized Jewry. Unwittingly, he has paid Judaism the finest compliment. After all, this fossilized Jewry has not been preserved "out of the way," deep down in the air-tight vault of a pyramid, but on all the storm-assailed highways of history. What a power this fossilized Judaism must possess if it succeeded in holding a fossilized Jewry together against the fury of nineteen centuries of inhumanity and barbarity! It must possess a secret source of inexhaustible energy, unknown to the empires and mighty conquerors that fossilized Jewry has outlasted. However, the compliment, even though very flattering, cannot be accepted, because the explanation of the survival of the fossil does not seem to make much sense. It sounds very much like a suggestion that the best way to preserve a mummy is to encase it in another mummy and then let it lie around to be kicked about and trampled upon by all. It is simple: mummy A converts itself into the appropriate "cement" in order "to hold together" mummy B. If one might give a broader currency to the Toynbean principle of fossil preservation, one might also say that the best way for a dead body to hold itself together—no matter what an unfriendly environment may do to it—is to feed itself with cadaver. The "explanation" that a fossilized Judaism converted itself into a "social cement" and thus preserved a fossilized Jewry in the Diaspora—even though Toynbeanism needs it badly—is nothing but pompous nonsense.

As to the Zionist crime, we recall that Zionism was described as something worse than all the persecutors of Jewry in all history: more evil than Nebuchadnezzar, Titus, Hadrian, the Spanish and Portuguese Inquisition, and even Nazism. Toynbee does not seem to notice that even from his own point of view such an observation is absurd. Criminality is not normally associated with fossils. Barbarity, far from being a mark of fossilization, is the manifestation of primeval, demoniac vitality. If Zionist Jewry "outnazied" the Nazis and out-persecuted Torquemadas, then Jewry must at least be tremendously alive.

One comes to the same conclusion as one looks more closely at Toynbee's application of the standards of the "Kingdom" to the Zionist guilt. The Jewish guilt is so overwhelming because the Jews, having suffered so much, knew what they were doing—whereas the Nazis, the Inquisitors, and the Hadrians did not. But, before making his accusation, Toynbee must surrender his previous interpretation that fossilized Jewry succeeded "in living without disaster" by rendering itself "insensible to the painfulness of the mundane Present by a minute observance of a God-given law. . . "[29] Only if they had felt what was done to them, could they have known better how to treat others. If Zionist Jewry is guilty, it must mean that it was fully conscious of what it was doing; there must have been a moment when it was faced with the challenge of the choice between "Good and Evil, Life and Death." But, as Toynbee so rightly maintains, a man is challenged by God and is able to choose Good and reject Evil by virtue of the freedom granted to him by God.[30] Therefore, if Zionist Jewry is guilty, it, too, must have been challenged by God and "set free" by Him to enable it to choose. How then could Jewry be a fossil? If the Zionist guilt surpasses the guilt of all other persecutors because Jewry, not having succeeded in rendering itself "insensible," had been vouchsafed "more light" by God in the experience of its own suffering, then surely Jewry must have been also more alive than all other persecutors. The greater challenge from God, the increase in responsibility, "more light" from God, are surely also manifestations of greater strength and richer vitality. We must then presuppose a Jewry that, far from having survived in the Diaspora in a state of fossilization by "living without disaster" on account of successful "insensibility," has been so eminently alive that it has survived in spite of disaster, living with it daily for endless centuries.

Thus Toynbee is back to his original problem: Jewry, which should have perished for rejecting the only path of salvation, lived on; having lived on, it survived centuries of oppression and martyrdom; having survived, it has returned to Zion, as it always said that it would do. All this has happened contrary to the Toynbean "laws" of history and against the "Will of God," as revealed in them according to Toynbee. The entire structure of the Toynbean universe is threatened with collapse. One may well sympathize with Mr. Toynbee. He is fighting, not very successfully, for his intellectual and spiritual survival. He is like the beggar whose garment is much too small to cover his body. Pull as he might, his nakedness will show.

VI. THE JEWISH DIASPORA AND JEWISH MESSIANISM

1. JUDAISM AND JEWRY IN EXILE

1.

IN THIS concluding chapter we shall attempt to offer a Jewish view of Jewish survival and Messianism, though only in outline, to set against the Toynbean discussion of the subject.

According to Toynbee Jewry should have produced a universal church, as befitted the internal proletariat at a Time of Troubles. But even in his view, the internal proletariat turns to religion for its peace only after it is let down by the creative minority. When the creative minority degenerates into the dominant minority, the internal proletariat refuses to follow and seeks its salvation in its own way.[1] But Jewry, as such, was never "charmed" by a Hellenic creative minority, and consequently it was not left without guidance and leadership when this creative minority degenerated into a dominant one. Jewry's spiritual home had never been Hellenism and, therefore, when —at the time of the disintegration of Hellenic civilization— the Hellenic dominant minority sought its redemption in the Romano-Hellenic universal state, Jewry was not spiritually homeless and did not have to look for shelter in the creation of a universal church.[2]

The creative minority of Jewry during the Maccabean and Zealot periods, and after, was the Pharisees. Notwithstanding the New Testament and Toynbee, they never degenerated into a dominant minority. They could not have done so, even if they had wanted to. As a result of their conflict with the Hasmonean princes, they were at first forced out of all positions of authority; later, from the time of Herod onward, following the policy of the revered Shemayah, they withdrew from all active association with the governing powers.[3] The Pharisees were neither priests nor clerics. They commanded no armies

116

and wielded no police powers; nor were they backed up by any state, either universal or national. They were men without office, who considered it against the Law to take remuneration either for teaching or for administering[4] and earned their living, like the rest of the people, in all kinds of trades and occupations. Some of them were rich; most of them, poor. They were lay teachers and lay preachers, the most distinguished and most representative laymen of their times. Being themselves of the people, they never deserted their people. Some of the publicans might well have followed Jesus; the people followed the Pharisees.

Far from being stiff-necked, inert, passive, and stubborn, they were alert, penetrating, conscious of the problems of their particular times, finding solutions in their own way. Thanks to them Jewry was saved. When Zealotism was crushed and the Herodians betrayed and deserted Jewry and the small sect of the Judeo-Christians betook itself to the refuge of their universal church, the Pharisees alone stood by the people and continued to teach them the art of survival. Nothing could be more inane than to suggest—as Toynbee says about Rabbi Johanan ben Zakkai—that they endowed Jewry with an "inertly rigid institutional frame-work" or that they admonished the people to seek the palladium of their preservation in the "social drill" of the "meticulous observance of the Mosaic Law." As we have seen, nothing is more dangerous to survival than rigidity and the unchangeable routine of social drill. The truth is that Judaism, as taught by the Pharisees, is not a meticulous observance of the Mosaic Law. The Sadducees, the opponents of the Pharisees and the people, alone represented the school of thought that insisted on the principle of the meticulous observance of the Mosaic Law. When, in the New Testament, the issue was raised of "the letter of the law that killeth," the Pharisees had already solved the problem. Theirs was, of course, not the Christian solution; but they had been aware of the issue long before the age of Jesus and had worked out an effective answer. The very purpose of the "Oral Law" of the Pharisees has been to make the Letter say what the Spirit would require it to say; the Pharisaic creation of the Halaha saved the Mosaic Law from ever becoming an "inertly rigid institutional framework," which would have surely rendered Jewry incapable of survival.[5] Rabbi Johanan ben Zakkai was indeed the man of destiny in the hour of the fall of Jerusalem; but, as we have already shown,[6] even this great master was a disciple who taught in the spirit of his teacher, Hillel. Far from endowing Jewry with rigidity and a passively obstinate psychological habitus, he was himself a leader of great flexibility, who rose to the challenge of a radically new situation with creativity of vision and boldness of decision and action. In the history of the Halaha, he is famous mainly for his "Tekanot," known as the "Reforms" of Rabbi Johanan ben Zakkai.[7] Even so, he does not represent a new departure in Judaism; he is only one link, though a very important one, in the long chain of Pharisaic tradition. He was creating and yet following precedence, and in doing so he was realizing the original purpose of the Halaha, which has always been to keep the Torah alive by applying it meaningfully to the changed conditions of every new age.

Spiritually and culturally Jewry was never a part of the "Hellenic" internal proletariat. The disintegration of the Hellenic civilization left the pagan section of that proletariat high and dry, but not Jewry. With the fall of Jerusalem the policies of some Jews were defeated, not Judaism. Only on the spiritual plane, in the soul of Jewry, could Judaism have been conquered; it is a feat that so far no civilization or religion has been able to accomplish. The fall of Jerusalem was naturally a tremendous challenge for Judaism and Jewry. Both survived because, thanks to the Pharisees, the challenge was met not unsuccessfully. Jewry has survived because it learned early that survival in itself is of little consequence; because by teaching and living, and often by the example of personal martyrdom, its Pharisaic creative minority was able to convince Jewry that man is living always in the presence of God and that his highest goal on earth is so to live that living itself, in all its manifestations, becomes the service of God. The destruction of the Jewish commonwealth by Titus was the loss of a specific "mundane" framework for Jewry's life; the Pharisees taught Jewry Judaism as a way of life that was not dependent for its survival on any specific external framework. For "let all thy deeds be done for the sake of Heaven"[8] really meant that no situation could ever arise in the life of a man in which he should not be able to fulfill his life purpose—to do the Will of his Father in Heaven as required of him by each passing moment and in whatever new place of his pilgrimage. No power on earth could change that. The decision is never with Titus or Hadrian or Torquemada or Hitler; it is always with a man's own conscience, and, therefore, always in a man's own hand.

2.

Considering the extremely unfavorable circumstances for Jewish survival, one cannot but acknowledge that the Pharisaic response to the challenge of the innumerable crises of Jewish history has been signally successful. One appreciates it fully only if one understands the ethos of Jewry in its various exiles. Jewry has certainly not survived "by an almost uncanny aptitude for economic specialization and a meticulous observance of jots and tittles of a traditional law."[9] Man does not live by commerce alone, nor does a people survive by ritualism. Man can of course not live without bread, and "the uncanny aptitude for economic specialization" might be considered a *conditio sine qua non* of Jewish survival. The aptitude had to be uncanny in response to the uncanny viciousness with which the dominant majority was continually sealing up every source of livelihood for the Jews; without the aptitude Jewry would have perished of starvation. But to fulfill a *conditio sine qua non* is not sufficient to survive; it cannot be the efficient cause for living and, certainly not, for enduring. As to ritualism, "the meticulous observance of jots and tittles," by now we have heard enough about Judaism to dismiss it. Decisive, however, is this consideration: while it might perhaps be conceivable for a community to survive by commerce and ritualism *if* it were left alone, Jewry has not been left alone for nineteen centuries. One does not walk to the burning stake for the sake of commerce and ritualism, and one certainly does not do it throughout "sixty generations." One cannot do it without a superior faith and an unshakable conviction, knowing that one is doing the Will of one's Heavenly Father.

The ethos of the Jewish Diaspora was not quietism, as Toynbee would have us believe. Martyrdom is not quietism; it is the highest form of activism. But for the Hitler era Jewish martyrdom was not just imposed upon the Jew by man's inhumanity; it was chosen and accepted by the Jew out of loyalty to his faith and ideals. The Jews could have stayed in the Spain of the Visigoths, just as they could have stayed in the Spain of Ferdinand and Isabel. There was the choice before them: either Judaism and the loss of home and property, and a life of exile and misery, or the acceptance of Christianity and peace and quietude and prosperity. The door of escape was always open before them: escape from "penalization" (to use Toynbee's euphemism), from discrimination, from the raping, pillaging, murdering bands of the Crusades, from the fury of the persecutions in a Europe driven to frenzied sadism by the overhanging shadow of the Black Death. The way of escape from the Pales and the Ghettos, from the eternal pogroms and blood libels, was always open. There was always the choice before Jewry; Christianity was ready to receive the Jews with open arms. The "first opportunity to persecute" did not arise for the Jews when the Zionists "conquered" the area of the Jewish state in Palestine "by the force of arms." For nineteen centuries Jews had been free to join the dominant majority in all the countries of the world; they could have become part of Western Christendom, which Toynbee calls the "arch-aggressor." Jews could have themselves become Visigoths, Spaniards, Germans, Poles, Russians; Torquemadas, Chmielnickis, Petluras. But they chose not to; they chose Judaism.

Countless times, in their tens of thousand, Jews chose "the plunge into the city waters" because—well, let Toynbee say why, in his own impressive words. A special form of "godlike enlightenment," he says, "inspired the confidence and fortitude that Jesus and Socrates and More displayed when they forbore to embrace opportunities held out to them for saving their lives at the price of compromising the truth which it was their mission to proclaim."[10] Indeed, it must have been some form of divine enlightenment that gave millions and millions of martyred Jews the fortitude to disregard the opportunities held out to them for saving their lives at the price of compromising the truth which it was, perhaps, not their *mission* to proclaim, but which constituted their life purpose.

3.

Jewry could have had it much easier. Toynbee is right in maintaining that, by refusing to recognize Jesus, "Judaism was renouncing its birthright in two great enterprises which eventually made the respective fortunes of two different daughters of Judaism": it was abandoning "the fallow and fertile missionfield of the Hellenic universal state to a Christian Church . . . driven into independence," and it was also "leaving to an Islam, whose founder was to be rebuffed by the Jewish Diaspora . . . the subsequent political task of reuniting a Syriac World."[11] A Jew will readily agree with this; but he would not call it a renunciation of Judaism's birthright. Judaism never considered "the making of fortunes" its birthright. It is quite possible that Judaism might itself have become a universal church and Jewry, the founder of a universal state; but at what price? Toynbee, for example, says that the triumph of Christianity was accomplished in "an Hellenic dress" by making concessions to polytheistic concepts, deeply ingrained in the mentality of the Hellenic society. Christianity triumphed over its competitors because by going "the greatest lengths in Hellenizing itself" it was able "to turn the flank of the resistance" which was offered to it by Hellenic paganism.[12] The case of the triumph of Islam was similar; it too had to incorporate many of the practices and beliefs of the heathen Arab tribes in order to convert them. In the final reckoning, victory and defeat, in the case of religions, are "not quite so different as would appear on the surface." Toynbee accepts the view, which he quotes, that "All religions, without exception, in order to overcome the obstacles that retarded their progress, have had to come to terms with the forces that they have been combating, and to succumb to some extent to the very evils against which it has been their mission, and indeed their raison d'être, to wage war..."[13] It is not unlikely that Jewry's Pharisaic creative minority well understood the "opportunities" that were offered to Judaism and saw in them temptations which had to be overcome. In their opinion, Judaism was not prepared to renounce its birthright for the kind of progress and triumph that required compromise with polytheism and paganism.[14] "What shall it profit a man if he shall gain the whole world and lose his own soul?"— the reckoning of spiritual values as expressed in this dictum was not unknown to the Pharisees.[15] One of the great Pharisaic teachers of the last pre-Christian centuries forwent high office, which was dependent on his retraction of some opinions of whose validity he was convinced, with the words: "It is better for me to be called a fool all the days of my life rather than to be a sinner before the Omnipresent, be it even only for a moment."[16]

Mr. Toynbee seems to give too much significance to success in history: the wicked perish and "the meek shall inherit the earth." Yes, but when? And what is perishing and what inheriting? He is deeply impressed by universal churches and overlooks the fact that in history the concept, like that of universal states, is a purely empirical one; it applies to a church or religion that has succeeded in gaining many adherents. But what does the concept express in terms of value or truth? The transfer of the Stone of Cybele to Rome was a great success, and the new cult based on the Holy Stone had many votaries. The theory that during the disintegration of a civilization the internal proletariat "secedes" in order to create a "universal" religion may or may not be correct. The event in itself, if it happens, proves nothing about the value of the universal religion thus established. It is useless to organize a plebiscite either about Truth or about God. If a religion is true, it is so, even though it be "unsuccessful"; if it is false, the conquest of the universe will not improve its quality.[17]

The Pharisees cared little for "success"; their concern was with the service of the One True God, as it was granted to them to understand Him and to serve Him. The choice was there before them from the very beginning—between the great "fortunes" that were to be made in the fallow fertile mission field of the Hellenic universal state and "being called a fool all one's life long rather than to be a sinner before the Omnipresent." In loyalty to their conscience, they renounced the fortunes and went into exile, though they might have inherited an empire. Their greatest achievement, however, was that they were able to persuade their own people to follow them. Their authority derived from the Word, their teaching, and their personal example. They organized Jewry for a life of sorrow and suffering in exile on the basis of a voluntarily accepted self-discipline. They imparted to Jewry an ethos that enabled it to maintain its organization, its institutions, its communal coherence, under conditions of political helplessness and without the enforcement of a "secular arm," normally essential for the maintenance of human society.[18] They imbued Jewry with the fortitude and conviction to renew its decision in face of the continuous challenge of its exile and to choose again and again "Life and Good" rather than the "great fortunes" of a passing day.

Thus exile has been the highest form of activism. The perennial "penalization" to which the Jewry of the Diaspora has been subjected represented a continuous challenge, which had to be answered daily. The unceasing pressure of enmity, discrimination, and persecution, a thousandfold intensified by the always-open avenue of escape by apostasy, required the unceasing renewal of Jewry's decision for Judaism. To live in exile has meant to affirm one's faith with every breath, from the first to the last. Exile has been a continuous "transference of action from the Macrocosm to the Microcosm," the "self-determination" of an entire people. While the others persecuted, Jews chose; and they chose God, as they understood Him. The "magnificent tragedy," so clearly recognized by Gregorovius in one event of Jewish history during the rule of the Roman procurators,[19] has been enacted on innumerable occasions in all the exiles of Jewry.

The ethos of Jewry in exile is epitomized in the prayer of an unknown Jew, one among the hundreds of thousands who chose to leave Spain in 1492 rather than accept Christianity.

With his family he crossed over to North Africa, where—like so many of his fellow refugees—he wandered about in desert lands, often going for days without food and water. When his wife and two children perished of exhaustion, he turned to God with these words: "Creator of the Universe! I know well that you have brought all this misery upon us in order to test and to try us. Know then that there is nothing you can do to us that could ever make us leave you."[20] How did they survive? No doubt, not forever will it remain a mystery.

2. JUDAISM AND MESSIANISM

1.

The Diaspora has always been considered by Judaism and Jewry a "temporary" condition—Galuth, i.e., exile. Tragedy, however magnificent, is not a normal form of human existence; the exile is a transitory form of Jewish life that is to pass as surely as it came. That Israel was destined to return to Zion has been part of the faith by which Jews have lived and endured through the ages. The belief in the return to Zion has been a manifestation of Messianism and until the era of Jewish emancipation an unquestioned cornerstone in the edifice of Judaism itself. Only in recent times have some assimilationist interpreters of Judaism attempted to dispense with it as being non-essential for Jewish monotheism.

In the context of our discussion one may well disregard the assimilationist interpretation, which—in any case—is of little significance in the light of the overwhelming testimony of Jewish history and of the authentic sources of Judaism.

Jewish Messianism is the direct outcome of Judaism itself. Toynbee is unable to understand it because he is so conditioned as to be unable to grasp an essential trait of Judaism. As a result of his "faith" in Original Sin and the hopelessness of salvation in "this World," he assumes that the Higher Religions address themselves to individual souls and not to societies. All salvation is "otherworldly"; nothing much worth while may really be done with "this World." This, of course, is a fairly well-known Christian position. However, he makes the serious mistake of assuming that Judaism was too "originally" charged with an "ecumenical *otherworldly* mission." Not being able to recognize the "ecumenical otherworldly mission" in long stretches of Jewish history, he maintains that Jewry itself betrayed Judaism by "transforming" it. And since for him it is a question of either otherworldly ecumenical salvation or else "this World" and the Mundane, Jewish Messianism, seeking to establish something in "this World," is but a parochial mundane enterprise.[21]

However, Toynbee was looking in vain for signs of Judaism's "otherworldly mission" in Jewish aspiration. Judaism does not have, nor did it ever have, such a mission. The "Kingdom of God" is a Judaic concept, and Jesus took it from Judaism; yet, when he declared that his Kingdom was not of this world, he was actually parting company with Judaism. Each of the Jewish daily services concludes with the same prayer for the establishment of the world as a Kingdom of God. The Torah is not in Heaven, because it is not needed in Heaven. It is here, in this world alone, that the Torah is relevant; the soul needs no commandments, the dead body is "free" from them. Only man, in whom Life and Death meet, is faced with the choice between "Life and the Good and Death and the Evil." The Kingdom of God is not given: it has to be built. This world is the raw material and man is the builder; as he chooses, so he builds. From the Jewish point of view, it is not an already extant Kingdom which is being revealed by the "renting of a veil," the mystery of Transfiguration; as far as man is concerned, the Kingdom has to be established by the *transformation* of this world through human endeavor. Of course, there can be no perfection in this world; but neither can there be perfection in any other world. Perfection is with God alone, and it is impossible outside and apart from Him. Therefore, the Kingdom is man's perennial challenge and his endless opportunity. "It is not for you to complete the work, but neither are you free to desist from it."[22]

That the Kingdom of God is to be erected by man in this world is reflected in the passage of Jeremiah in which we have already recognized the summation of Judaism's system of values. Let it stand here once more:

> Thus saith the Lord:
> Let not the wise man glory in his wisdom,
> Neither let the mighty man glory in his might,
> Let not the rich man glory in his riches;
> But let him that glorieth glory in this,
> That he understandeth, and knoweth Me,
> That I am the Lord who exercise mercy,
> Justice and righteousness, in the earth;
> For in these things I delight,
> Saith the Lord.[23]

It is important to understand that this concept refers not to the kingdom of utilitarian ethics; not to the peace secured by the arm of Caesar, nor the justice upheld in the court of law alone; not to the righteousness of social respectability, nor a form of universal reconciliation imposed upon mankind, perhaps, by the universal fear of atomic destruction. Nothing is further from Judaism than the thought that the Kingdom of God could be brought about merely by the external control of human conduct.[24] Such control is necessary as a way of preparation. The task is not an easy one. It requires living with the continuous awareness of God's Presence; it needs continuous reminders, a system of self-discipline that will help a man gradually to gain control over the powerful temptations of his self-centeredness. The Kingdom of God is established by man's imitation of God. What Jeremiah conveys is that God's own concern, as far as it calls for man's attention, is with this world, with the exercise of "mercy, justice, and righteousness in the earth." The knowledge of the Lord, which is the highest virtue, is to know that "in these things" He delights, and the imitation of God is to "imitate" Him in the exercise of these things out of "delight."

2.

It follows from such a position that man is not saved by faith alone; decisive is the deed of transformation, the deed that issues from faith and, because of that, transforms man and his

126

life. But man is never alone in the world, and his life is inter-linked with all Life. Building the Kingdom is a "public" act; it is an event that occurs always in a "society." If a man's deed of transformation is to be effective, he must make common cause with those of his fellow men who are closest to him, who are most immediately affected by his life, and whose behavior, in turn, affects him most directly. The smallest cell of the Kingdom is a society. One may also put it this way: the world as a whole is to be made into the Kingdom. Salvation therefore aims not at man, but—through man—at mankind. But one cannot begin with mankind. Though mankind may be a reality "in the Spirit," in reality it is an ideal to be striven for. We are all brothers—potentially. In reality, we have yet to *become* brothers. The salvation of mankind is its establishment. One does not create mankind with mankind: one does it with men. One begins with oneself and in the narrower society to which one belongs by the destiny of birth. The Kingdom realized posits mankind as a whole; but in history, the progress of its realization always begins "at home."

The "society" which we have called the smallest cell of the Kingdom of God may be of varied size; but the richer the manifestations of its life, the greater the challenge and the richer the opportunities for transformation. Judaism looked upon Jewish peoplehood as an opportunity for more effective and more significant transformation. The acceptance of Juda-ism by Jewry meant that the life of an entire people was to be transformed into a province of the Kingdom. The manifesta-tions of individual, family, and social life within the nation, individual and social ethics, the administration of justice, politi-cal decisions—all were to be informed with the purposes of the Kingdom; individual as well as national behavior was to be determined by the religious faith of the community. This is meant by the words: "and ye shall be unto Me a kingdom of priests, and a holy nation." Neither nationhood nor kingdom is an end in itself; they are both transcended by a life whose function is "priesthood" and whose goal is holiness.

It is for this reason that Judaism requires not only a people but also a land for its realization. A soul that finds its salvation in otherworldly grace needs no this-worldly home; but a people that aspires to the building of the Kingdom on earth needs its corner on earth wherein to build it. A Jew would not agree with Toynbee's opinion that the highest form of society is a universal church. From the Jewish point of view, the highest form of society is a religious civilization that strives to establish its own structure, in all its organizational and institutional manifestations, with a view to furthering the transformation of this world into the Kingdom of God. And the "this world" of a people, for the practical purpose of building the Kingdom, is its homeland. For this reason, the land of Israel is essential for the faith of Israel.

In all its rawness and dark, demoniac wildness, this world is extremely precious for man's salvation. The Spirit as such, in the realm of human existence, lacks efficacy. Faith alone will not move mountains; but faith will move mountains if it has hands and bodies and machines at its command.[25] The physical, the material, the "mundane" are indispensable for the Spirit, if it wishes to take effect in this world. Only through the instrumentality of the Material can the conscious aspiration of the Spiritual find expression and realization in the life of men. A man cannot even think goodness without a brain; he can certainly not do good without a body. All energy and power in this world has its seat in the material and organic ground of life; all purpose and value, in its spiritual manifestation. The Purposeful, on its own, is powerless; the Powerful, by itself, purposeless. The greatest waterfall, left to itself, will only fall; the finest blue print, left in the drawer of the engineer, will not move a single wheel. The two realms find their salvation in their "interpenetration." The Spirit alone may redeem the Mundane from its blind demoniac purposelessness; the Mundane alone may reciprocate by offering liberation to the Spirit from the prison of its powerlessness.[26] The two realms meet in man; and in their interpenetration, through man, this world is transformed into the Kingdom of God. By investing the Mundane with value and significance and the Spirit with power and effectiveness, the act of interpenetration becomes the sanctification of life.

A people that sees its destiny in striving for the sanctification of life needs a holy land for its religious-spiritual fulfillment. As the Kingdom of God in its universal Messianic realization requires the world for its place, so does Judaism require the land of Israel for the implementation of its own contribution to the Kingdom. Exile is therefore not only a material but also a spiritual catastrophe for Jewry. The separation between Torah and Zion is always a spiritual tragedy. This tragedy is well illustrated by the example that Toynbee uses to describe the "Diffraction of Culture." A well-integrated culture he compares to a flint, in which the many constituent "flakes" have been "compacted by the age-long pressure of enormous forces." The nucleus of a culture may be its religion; the various "flakes" which surround the nucleus are the economic, political, and cultural planes of life. In the process of disintegration the various flakes are split away from the core one by one, until the religious nucleus is exposed. "This religious quintessence of a culture is perhaps proof against disintegration, but it is not proof against stultification through being isolated from all the other activities of Life and thereby being inhibited from exercising the pervasive influence which Religion is able to exercise in a healthily integrated body social."[27] Jewry's exile is not a healthily integrated body social, nor could it ever be. Judaism becomes stultified for lack of opportunity for "interpenetration" with the economic, political, social, and cultural "flakes" which "a demonic flintknapper" has forcibly broken away from it. Judaism is inseparable from the Jewish land; nor has the people of Judaism ever severed its link with the land. The striving for realization calls for the return to Zion.

3.

Because the building of the Kingdom is a "social" endeavour that always starts "at home," a somewhat puzzling paradox is bound to arise. The actual "society" in history is always a specific one. It will be distinguished by time and place, which are unique for each of the larger societies; by language, custom, and interest; by the specific case of its own "rawness," which has yet to be "transformed"; and even by the specific way and method by which it attempts the responsibility of transforming itself into a province of the Kingdom. However, the actual kingdom, in its state of realization, which is the ultimate goal, is essentially universal. It is therefore a distinctive group, distinctive in its rawness as well as in its approach to the challenge of transformation, which strives for the realization of the all-embracing, universal Kingdom of God. There is no other path in history: the people of God cannot but be a "peculiar" people—a distinctive national group charged with a universal responsibility. That this responsibility is not discharged by going out into the world to preach a gospel, but by staying at home to live a gospel, only intensifies the challenge. The group distinctiveness of the "peculiar" people is the ever-menacing pitfall for its universal responsibility. Yet, there is no other way. The Kingdom of God has to be built, and one has to start building it in one's own corner of the universe. The "peculiar" people, which through its universal responsibility learns that nationhood is only a means to the Kingdom, must look upon itself as a universal people, whose distinctiveness must be turned into the distinguishing mark of one branch of an all-embracing humanity.

Such a philosophy, far from making Jewry an exclusive community, actually links its destiny as closely as possible to the destiny of the rest of the world. The communion of saints may take place in isolation; a soul may be saved in an "otherworldly" miracle of Grace, while the rest of mankind may be damned. But the Kingdom of God, which consists in the transformation of this world, involves everybody in the destiny of everybody else. Since no one can do more than to build the Kingdom in his own corner, in his own sphere of influence, this world will become the Kingdom of God as a result of cooperation and increasing reconciliation among all men and all "peculiar" people. Therefore, the prophets of Israel never visualized the redemption of Israel as an isolated event in history but as one that will come about, "at the end of the days," within the general redemption of all mankind. The Pharisees gave expression to the interdependence of all human salvation in history when, applying the prophetic tradition to the exile of Israel, they said: "Every misfortune in which Israel and the nations share as partners is a genuine misfortune; but one that is Israel's alone, is not a genuine misfortune."[28] Israel's exile has lasted so long because it is a genuine tragedy; it indicates how far removed this world still is from the Kingdom of God. Jewry cannot be redeemed without the redemption of the nations; nor will the nations be redeemed without the redemption of Israel. "They shall not hurt nor destroy in all My holy mountain; for the earth shall be full of the knowledge of the Lord, as the waters cover the sea."[29]

3. ZIONISM

Zionism should not be identified with Messianism. Jewish Messianism is an expression of Judaism; it is the general faith that, notwithstanding the failures and backslidings of Jews as well as of the rest of mankind, the Kingdom of God will yet be a reality in this world. Zionism, on the other hand, is composed of particular forces, needs, and longings in Jewish life.

Let us attempt to indicate the components of modern Zionism. The most obvious element seems to be the practical need of the Jewish people. Whatever the higher aspirations of Judaism, and whatever the functions and destiny of Jewry in world history, Jews are people: they are human beings. Like other people they do not enjoy being pushed about, persecuted, and chased from country to country. They have been homeless for nineteen centuries, and all the time they were longing for the home that had been theirs but had been taken from them. One does not commit a crime, nor does one embrace the idolatry of nationalism, merely by seeking protection against the inhumanity of "penalization." Perhaps the majority of the Jews who now live in the Jewish state were *driven* to Erets Israel by Christian as well as Arab nations.

In addition, there has been the *moral* need. A people is not a mere aggregate of individuals. It possesses not only a biological but also a psychological and spiritual coherence. A people has distinctiveness, an identity of its own. Like everything else that is alive, it wants to live on. A people needs a home for itself. There is no reason why the Jewish people should not have felt this need—should not have the right, like all other peoples, to satisfy it. For the solution of the present serious crisis of the Western world, Mr. Toynbee suggests not the dissolution of nationalities—the disappearance of the English, French, Germans, Russians, and so on—but "a middle way between two mutually antithetical deadly extremes: a devastating strife between irreconcilable parochial states and a desolating ecumenical peace imposed through the delivery of a knock-out blow." Or, as he calls it, "the saving harmony of multiplicity-in-unity and unity-in-multiplicity."[30] It is a goal to which Zionism can sincerely subscribe. But what is right for the nations of the West and the East cannot be wrong only because it is claimed on behalf of the Jewish people. If the idolatry of nationalism is correctly defined "as a spirit which makes people feel and act and think about a part of any given society as though it were the whole of that society,"[31] then to deny the Jewish people the chance to preserve its identity, to continue to live and to express itself by way of its selfhood, is "to feel and act and think about a part of a given society" as if it were dead—or at least ought to be dead.

Apart from the material need of the Jews and the moral need of the Jewish people, there have also been in Zionism rich veins of noblest idealism. One of the finest types that have appeared on the stage of modern history has been that of the Haluts, the Zionist pioneer. Young men and women by the thousand left the cities and ghettos of Europe to devote their lives to the redemption of a land ravaged by centuries of neglect, in order to redeem a people crushed to the ground by centuries of human hatred. The people was their people and the land was the land of their fathers. The Haluts went to Palestine not in order to fight with other human beings, but ready to give his life—as he actually did—in an aweinspiring struggle with the swamps and the deserts and the malaria of a devastated country. Moved by idealism, he went there with the determination to build a better, a juster, and a more humane society than the one he had left behind in Europe. No doubt the Haluts often went to

Palestine feeling a rich measure of Toynbean disillusionment with the "West." Having repeatedly experienced the impact of Western barbarity on his own body, his soul was longing for a creative life of self-sacrifice which alone could cleanse him of the contaminating burden of abominable memories. One of the early Halutsim wrote in a letter after a pogrom in the Pale, the Toynbean "homeland" of the Jews: ". . . if we do not find something to *redeem* us from this horror we shall go mad."[32] And he went to Palestine. Very likely he perished of hunger and malaria, as so many of the early Halutsim did; but not before he had redeemed his soul from the demoralizing stranglehold of the horror that he had seen.

Besides such secular idealism and longing for "secular salvation," one of the motivating forces within Zionism is Jewry's longing for Messianic salvation. From its inception, outstanding religious leaders and broad sections of religious Jewry have identified themselves with the Zionist movement. They did not substitute Zionism for Messianism, but they recognized in Zionism a movement that subserved the aspirations of Messianic Judaism. There was indeed a great deal of secularism in the Zionist movement, which religious Jews rejected and against which they fought. But they could not overlook the purity of the motivation of so many of their "secularist" brothers and sisters. The secularism in Zionism emphasized for them the nature of their responsibility, which was, as it has always been, to strive for the sanctification of the secular, not by preaching and finding fault with others, but by transforming this world into the Kingdom, first of all in one's own corner. Especially for the religious Zionist, Jewry's exile was also the spiritual tragedy of the stultification of Judaism; the "flakes" had been broken away from the core of the flint. The return to Zion alone promised the gradual reintegration of the body social, within which the task of "interpenetration" could be taken up anew. Religious Zionism recognized that the upbuilding of Palestine was the opportunity, as well as the inescapable challenge, to work through the redemption of the people for the redemption of Judaism itself.

There is, however, one important element in the debacle of

the West which one does not find in Zionism—a Master Race ideology. No doubt modern nationalism had great influence on the Zionist movement, but not every form of nationalism is Fascism or Nazism. Nor would it have been possible for Zionism to accomplish so much if it had been a mere imitation of a Western blunder. Zionism translated the needs and the sorrow of the Jewish people as well as the faith and the longings of the Jewish soul into a creative response to the challenge of the exile. The technique of political action and propaganda it might have learned from modern nationalism; the international recognition of the rights of oppressed national minorities encouraged Zionists to believe that what had been granted to others could not readily be denied to Jews. The need and the sorrow, the faith and the longing, were nineteen centuries old; it was they that through the ages had sustained Israel's hope for its eventual return to Erets Israel. In spite of exile, the link between the people and its land had never been severed. The continuity of Jewish history and the consistency in Jewry's aspirations were the foundation on which Zionism built; they were also the source of the idealism, of the moral energies of perseverance and self-sacrifice, ingenuity and heroism, without which the state of Israel could never have been established.

Unfortunately, there is no history, as there is no life, without some measure of guilt; and thus there is guilt associated with Zionism. However, it is guilt broadly distributed. First, there is the infamous guilt of sixteen centuries of Western barbarity against the Jews; and, while it is perhaps true that the Moslem world has been less guilty than the West, there is also the Moslem guilt of thirteen centuries of anti-Jewish discrimination and "penalization," of having reduced the Jew in most Arab countries to the status of the pariah. Without the impetus provided by the persecutors Zionism might never have succeeded. Then, there is the guilt of Great Britain: not for allowing Jews to settle in Palestine in conformity with the decision of the League of Nations, which—even though not the guardian angel of an "otherworldly" Kingdom of God—was at the time the highest international authority on earth; but for the cynically calculating imperialistic policy of *divida et impera,* the crime of the mandatory administration which for most of the thirty-odd years of its authority did everything in its power to widen the breach between Jew and Arab. There is the Jewish guilt for not having been able to reach an amicable settlement with the Arabs—as there is also the guilt of a barren Arab nationalism that did not permit any such understanding.

There is also the tragedy of the Arab-Jewish war, and in a war no one is innocent. But, apart from the Arab-Jewish guilt in the war, born of mutual fear and mutual distrust, there is the share in this guilt of those who had to fear nothing except the loss of some power and influence and who, for the sake of political considerations, did nothing to prevent the war. There is again the guilt of Great Britain, which having submitted the Palestine question to arbitration by the United Nations, refused to co-operate in the implementation of the U.N. decision and withdrew from Palestine, leaving behind planned chaos and confusion, hoping to be called back again to restore order and peace. There is also the shameful guilt of those forces that out of enmity for a state of Israel were urging on the Arabs to resist the authority of the United Nations, by force of arms.

And thus the responsibility for the plight of the Arab refugees is shared by many. It is part of the guilt of the war and of everything else that preceded it from the day that Jewry went into exile; but it has been aggravated a thousandfold by those who, having with shameless calculation turned human suffering into a pawn in the game of international power politics, prevent any constructive solution of this tragic problem.

Nothing is easier than to blame the Jews; nor is there anything cheaper than that. Today, as in the past, it is a sign of moral bankruptcy.

VII. EPILOGUE: ZERO HOUR

"... at a Zero Hour when all is sin and shame ..."
Toynbee, *A Study of History,* IV/584.

1.

A JEW who has finished reading Mr. Toynbee's ten bulky volumes cannot help wondering whether the results of his running battle against Judaism and Jewry could be greatly satisfying even to the author himself. If Judaism, having started out as an ecumenical religion of human salvation, ran into a blind alley, only to perish as the "social cement" of a fossilized Jewry, who—one might be curious to know—has fared any better? The question is of genuine significance, for one best understands the nature of a failure if one is able to compare it with its successful opposite.

In the category to which the Western society belongs, it appears that some fourteen civilizations have perished. Of the others of the same species, the Islamic, the Eastern, and the Far Eastern, though still extant, are "almost certainly in *articulo mortis*";[1] they are all stricken, and their final disappearance seems to be only a matter of time. Only the "West" is left—and unfortunately not in a very healthy state either. As a result of its secularization the West has gone through a Second Fall; it has become the votary of a neo-paganism or neo-barbarism that threatens its own destruction from within.[2] Here, as so often in Toynbee's work, it is not clear why he should be so hard on modern Western secularism, pretending at times that all was well with the West before the rise of European enlightenment and rationalism. Quite frequently, he dates the symptoms of "social breakdown" in the Western world from the sixteenth-century wars of religion. Secularism arose in reaction to the disappointing failure of religion.[3] We recall his discussion with the Western rationalist, quoted above. There Toynbee actually confirmed the dismal failure of the Higher Religions in deter-

mining human behavior in history, by defending them with
the argument that the six thousand years of civilization were
an extremely short period, for one ought to measure history
with the time-scale of modern physical and astronomical science. There is still so much time before the human race that
one should withhold judgment.[4] Thus it is obvious that the
record of the pre-secular centuries is not a very encouraging
one either.[5] Be that as it may, in view of the doubtful achievements of Western civilization, Toynbee himself applies to this
lonely survivor of the species[6] the familiar lines from "The
Ancient Mariner":

> The many men so beautiful!
> And they all dead did lie:
> And a thousand thousand slimy things
> Lived on: and so did I.

Now, the rather unpleasant survivor has already been overtaken by the "ominous symptoms" of disintegration. True, one
may derive hope from the fact that at this juncture Western
society has "certainly not yet arrived at the second rally in the
disintegration-process" which is always recognizable by the
"establishment of a Pax Ecumenica"; the universal state,
which as a rule comes about before the final dissolution of a
civilization, has not yet been established in the West.[7] However, just such a threat overhangs the Western horizon. The
progress of modern technology, especially the newly acquired
insight into the secret of atomic structure which gave Western
civilization the atom bomb, may enable one great power to
establish the unity of the ecumene with one knockout blow.
Actually, Toynbee might have pointed out, two knockout
blows by two opposing great powers may bring about the dissolution of Western society in one world-wide conflagration,
without the old-fashioned, roundabout method of going
through the sacrificial ceremony of first establishing a universal state. The knockout blow, this time, would have truly
universal consequences; for the process of "Westernization"
has by now reached all the corners of the earth. All mankind
has become involved in the destiny of the West; "all Mankind's

eggs had been gathered into one precious yet precarious basket as a consequence of the Western Civilization's World-wide expansion."[8] The situation is precarious because, as a result of the concentration of power, the direct outcome of relentless technological progress leaves only the Soviet Union and the United States to decide the issue upon which the future of man depends.

The present situation of the Western society is not altogether different from that of the Hellenic civilization before its final collapse. As then, so today, the crisis will be resolved not by political arrangements but by Man's relations with God, his Savior. Once again Toynbee affirms that "the most adroit and opportune political engineering applied to the structure of a body social could never serve as a substitute for the spiritual redemption of souls." All crucial questions of the present crisis are religious ones.[9] But the future is not without hope. It would appear that, after all, this Western secularized, neo-pagan neo-barbarian did do a few things not too badly. He abolished slavery in the nineteenth century; he granted independence to India; he is approaching the final solution of the Negro problem in America. Our secularist neo-pagan has done all this thanks "to the continuing operation of a spirit of Christianity that had not lost its hold over the hearts of latter-day Western men and women when their minds had eventually rejected an outworn creed in which the abiding spiritual truths of Christianity had been translated into the ephemeral language of a pagan Hellenic philosophy."[10] This "operation of a spirit of Christianity" is the great advantage that the West possesses over the Hellenic world, which for the lack of it had to perish. Having accomplished so much, may not Western man hope one day to abolish war too, the only remaining threat to his survival?

One is somewhat puzzled by this turn in Toynbean thinking. The modern West has done so many things wrong because it is neo-pagan; it has done quite a few things well because it is Christian. In fact, the neo-barbarian West seems to be more truly Christian than its Christian medieval predecessor was. In a sense, it has liberated "the abiding spiritual truths of Christianity" from the shell of an "outworn creed" in which they were imprisoned by "the ephemeral language of a pagan Hellenic philosophy."

Be that as it may, whilst there is hope nothing may be taken for granted. The progress of technology, which makes the threat to the future truly universal, contains also the potential for equally universal well-being. Perhaps most important of all, this progress has pushed the idea of a democratic world government within the scope of logical feasibility. But, as always, growth is from within. The "ripe fruits of Technology could not be harvested without a change of heart"; alas, of that "there was little sign" so far.[11] Therefore, the patient's prospects are "still enigmatic." Neither a dogmatic optimism nor a dogmatic pessimism is warranted. Everything seems to hang in the balance, and the future cannot be foretold.[12]

What then is to be done? What is the right deed that will save man? True to his main theme, Toynbee maintains that an act of reconversion is required of Western souls; man has to start out on "a fresh quest for the divine Dweller in the Innermost." This may be also the answer to Communism, for "the idol Leviathan might still be triumphantly defied and defeated by souls contending for the liberty of Conscience and risking martyrdom for the glory of God."[13] These are noble thoughts, nobly expressed. It is rather a pity that they should require implementation in the life of man. As we have learned by now, man is—unfortunately—not a very reliable creature; he cannot save himself. If the future of our Westernized planet depended on man alone, our imminent destiny would be "Death and not Life." But since we have no reason to assume that "God's nature is less constant than man's, we may and must pray that a reprieve which God has granted to our society once will not be refused if we ask for it again in a contrite spirit and with a broken heart."[14] It is important to understand how Toynbee imagines the new reprieve for which man must pray. He does not require Western man to return to the "old-time religion." It would be neither morally nor intellectually defensible for a post-Christian Western society to seek refuge from the impending storm in "the fold of a conventional Christian

orthodoxy." Such a return to the universal church would be a
form of religious archaism, but archaism is always a trap and
never a solution. Toynbee quotes and affirms the opinion that
there is no hope in returning to a traditional faith after it has
once been abandoned; "souls that have once had the experience of intellectual enlightenment can never thereafter find
spiritual salvation by committing intellectual suicide."[15]

The Western agnostic has been disillusioned by agnosticism
and rationalism, which have led him to the very brink of the
abyss. He is on "the road back to Religion from Agnosticism"
but must desist the temptation of running for shelter to one of
the universal churches; it is his duty to ride out the storm. He
must not forget that he is an "ex-agnostic." He is penitent and
contrite in spirit, but he cannot return to the fold because in
the Christian Church Christianity has become "a petrified
higher religion." He is so deeply sorry for his past apostasy that
his heart is filled with bitterness against those who share with
him the responsibility for it; but "the responsibility for Modern
Western Man's apostasy was shared with the apostate by a
Western Christian Church that had eventually alienated its
long-suffering votaries by its grievous sins of both heart and
head." Thanks to the moral scandal of the savage Western wars
of religion and the intellectual scandal of the reaction of a
Western Church Militant to the movement of intellectual enlightenment, "the Western Church had forfeited Western
Man's esteem." If the "ex-agnostic" went astray, it was because
"The diseased have ye not strengthened, neither have ye healed
that which was sick. . . ." The ex-agnostic and the Church will
never meet. God will judge both "the unfaithful shepherds and
truant sheep"; in the meantime "a change of heart was required on both sides." "Purification" is needed, "a winnowing
the chaff out of the wheat."

Neither the Church nor the "semi-penitent" agnostic is equal
to such a task. In the opinion of Toynbee, "a petrified higher
religion could not be requickened by methods that might serve
for reconditioning an obsolete industrial plant. A futuristic reconstruction of Christianity by reconverted agnostics and an
archaistic restoration of it by trustees of a traditional orthodoxy

would both be impracticable for the same reason; and the reason was that no human hands could anticipate the operation of the Holy Spirit."[16]

The purification, the change of heart, will have to be the result of the operation of the Holy Spirit itself; once again it is affirmed that God alone is Savior. What Toynbee expects is a new Divine Epiphany. Modern man is passing through the Western society's second bout of its Time of Troubles, which according to the rule could end in salvation only through the emergence of a universal religion. One should look forward to a new revelation, even to a new religion. Toynbee actually says so, when he suggests that the conflict between the remaining great powers, the Soviet Union and the United States, provides "a supreme opportunity for an act of spiritual creation by evangelists who came to bring, not a sword, but peace." The aim must be not to make the one prevail over the other, "but in seeking to make the challenge of an encounter yield the response of a new spiritual vision opening up the vista of a new way of life."[17] The present situation is parallel to the situation in Judea at the time of the conflict between Judaism and the invading Hellenic civilization; as then, so now, salvation lies in evangelism alone.[18] As then, so today, a new vision is required to transcend both parties to the conflict and to unite them on a higher spiritual plane. Evangelism and the new vision stem always from the direct intervention of the Holy Spirit.

With all this, we come back to our starting point: What is the task of man at Zero Hour? What has he to do? We have already heard that he has to repent, to pray, and to be of contrite spirit. The most important duty, however, is to imitate Jesus through the acceptance of suffering.[19] As always, suffering is the key to salvation. It is in suffering that God reveals Himself to man. We have to work our way "from Trouble to Truth." Toynbee quotes: "New faiths, like children, must be born in sorrow, and many souls will have to pass through struggles greater than they can bear. . . ." This is the Toynbean testament. Mankind will be saved, if saved it will be, through a new faith, born of the union of human sorrow and "the operation of the Holy Spirit." Neither can we nor dare we anticipate the nature of the future revelation. Man must cling and suffer and wait patiently for the Lord, trusting in His grace. And so the testament concludes with a quotation from the Jewish Psalms: "Purge me with hyssop, and I shall be clean."[20]

2.

One cannot but be moved by these manifestations of the spiritual travail of a human soul. The bitter disillusionment of the ex-agnostic with man, which has led him back to God but not yet to religion, proves what he set out to disprove, namely, that human history has been "nasty, brutish, and short."[21] That Hobbes was right when he penned those pessimistic words is born out by the *A Study of History;* that he may yet be proved wrong, thanks to God's love for man, is Toynbee's hope and faith. *A Study of History* is a devastating account of the inadequacy of man. Toynbee formulates the problem but knows no answer. He does not run for refuge to a church; he does run to God. Far be it from us to blame him for that. However, his clinging to God is not a solution, but an escape— an escape from the terrible vision of the historian. No wonder therefore that at Zero Hour he has nothing positive to offer as a contribution to the solution of the present crisis of man.

That man is a problematic creature we have known for a long time; that he ought to be good and believe in God and repent and pray and be of a contrite spirit is no new discovery either. The problem has always been how to *change* man. Toynbee says that only God can change him through the mystery of Transfiguration. But, according to Toynbee, God has done it at least once; unfortunately, the success was neither long enduring nor very convincing. A handful of saints have been produced, but man in the mass remained subject to the sway of Original Sin; and today we are perhaps worse off than we have ever been before, if one may judge by the new outbursts of human criminality in modern history and by what is now threatening the future of the human race. Toynbee's advice is: Imitate Jesus and accept suffering; through suffering you will be reborn and saved. Actually, the older advice that man should be good and virtuous was not bad either. It would be a very good thing indeed if people imitated Jesus. But, alas, Toynbee forgets to say how people might be moved to accept suffering as a personal sacrifice for the sake of their salvation. In order to be able to act, in mass, on the Toynbean advice, they must be reborn first—in which case, of course, the advice would become superfluous.

However, apart from this general consideration, Toynbee lets us down badly in his final message. What does he mean by the acceptance of suffering and waiting for God? Shall we abolish hospitals and stop curing diseases? Shall we give up modern hygiene, forego the amenities of modern civilization? Shall we live on herbs and roots instead of steak? Shall we all become ascetics? It is unlikely that this is his message. The imitation of Jesus could have only one meaning, to act as Jesus acted: not to resist evil; to reject conquest by the sword, even though one is sure to be victorious with the sword;[22] to do what, as we saw, the Maccabees and the Zealots failed to do, to live by the ethos of gentleness; to go out into the world to conquer souls by submitting to suffering, imposed by others, as did the Israelitish exiles in Babylon and the primitive Christians in the disintegrating Hellenic society. The present crisis, says Toynbee, is the "supreme opportunity" for evangelism; but he fails to go on and say: In the conflict with a materialistic Communism let us turn into the path that alone may lead to salvation; let us destroy our weapons, throw away our atom bombs; let us beware of repeating the tragic error of the Maccabees and the satanic Jewish Zealots of resisting force with force. If as a result of such an attitude Communism should conquer the world, what does it really matter? The conflict between Communism and the West is a secular as well as a religious drama, "an otherworldly mystery play"; but "from the religious standpoint of the preachers of spiritual salvation the secular drama is a vanity of vanities."[23]

Toynbee fails shamefully by not having the moral courage to apply the logical outcome of his entire thesis to the present situation, to translate the terms of his very vehement criticism of the Maccabees and Jewish Zealots into a clarion call to the conscience of present-day Christendom. If his ten volumes have any meaning, they should have caused him to turn to the Western democracies, or at least to the confessedly Christian countries, with a manifesto: Know ye then that all who take the sword shall perish by the sword. Turn your atomic piles into peaceful uses. Submit to Communist domination meekly and accept suffering, for suffering is the key to salvation. Remember that "the gospel of Christianity is not addressed to societies but to souls; and any soul in any social environment is a potential convert to the way of salvation."[24] Had he spoken thus, one might still not have had to accept his philosophy or theology, but one could have respected him for the courage of his convictions. But Toynbee does not have such courage. The travail of his soul produces the wisdom: Let us suffer and wait for the Lord, but let us also keep our powder dry for all eventualities. What then does he mean by the acceptance of suffering? Apparently, the spiritual travail of the soul, derived from the heroic perusal of the annals of human history. Mr. Toynbee is like the great diver, who explores the depth of all the oceans; believing that he has at last succeeded in wresting from them their innermost secret, he comes to the surface—with a handful of glittering sand.

3.

As for the Jewish student who concludes a study of Toynbee, he cannot but feel deeply embarrassed. He realizes that to have failed and to be a fossil are not really dishonorable. More than fourteen higher civilizations have already perished. Those still extant are badly stricken; the only one with a certain, not-very-well-explained hope for survival is—as Mr. Toynbee attests—a somewhat "slimy thing." The four "living" Higher Religions too seem to be all "petrified." In view of the fact that for sixty generations Jewry—as again certified by Mr. Toynbee himself—remained free of the guilt of aggression and persecution, which during the same time has been piling up to tragically towering heights on the backs of Toynbee's "living" religions and civilizations, the present writer must confess that many a time, during his study, he was "tempted to offer the Pharisee's thanksgiving":[25] Ribbono shel Olam! If this is being alive, I thank Thee with all my heart for having made me a fossil. He must also confess that, in view of the fact that to fail and to perish and to become petrified seem to be the norm in history, and salvation to be the mysterious miracle of exception, the venom of Mr. Toynbee's condemnation of Jewry, and the vehemence of his rejection of Judaism, for having failed where greater and mightier societies and religions have not succeeded either, seemed to be out of all proportion to the Jewish share in man's failure in history. Mr. Toynbee's offensive and deliberately humiliating treatment of both Judaism and Jewry must be understood as a desperate attempt to stifle a suspicion in his own heart that, perhaps, there might be something right with Judaism after all.

Concerning the present crisis of the West, the Jewish student of *A Study of History* is even more embarrassed to find that the decisive issues of Zero Hour are directly or indirectly related to Judaism and Jewry. The two colossi, facing each other in the present crisis of mankind, have conflicting ideologies; but these ideologies take their origin from two great personalities who, though antithetical, were nevertheless Jews. A Jew, Jesus, was the founder of Christianity and a Jew, Karl Marx, the founder of the Marxian philosophy of dialectical materialism. The conflict between the colossi is charged with a potential threat to the human race owing to the progress of modern physical science, which placed in human hands unlimited powers of possible destruction. But the era of modern science is dominated by one outstanding name, that of a Jew, Albert Einstein. Without the Einsteinian physics the release of atomic energy would not be conceivable. The two opposing ideologies and modern, relativistic science dominate the entire contemporary situation. A Jew is able to recognize in each of the three a specific expression of a basic Jewish concept, namely, that of "Ehad," of Unity. The Unity that Judaism affirms of God implies the unity of the One God's creation. Faith in the One God posits the unity of mankind as well as the unity of physical nature. The unity of physical nature has to be discovered by man, that of mankind established by him. The Marxian doctrine is a unifying philosophy, in that it aims at the establishment of a politically unified humanity in a Kingdom of Man that is identical with "this World." Christianity is a unifying religion that aims at the salvation of all mankind in a Kingdom of God that is not of "this World." On the other hand, the unlimited power wielded by the two colossi, threateningly as well as promisingly, is the result of modern science, which owes its unparalleled progress to the unifying force of the relativity theory, which discovered the "oneness" of mass and energy and explains both through the curvature of space.

At the same time, a Jew sees himself related to the most tragic debacle of Western society, i.e., fiendish Nazism. He notes that the essence of Nazism was a rebellion against the principle of unity, aiming, as it did, at the establishment of a dualistic world order of rulers and ruled, masters and slaves. In its rebellion against the principle of unity, Nazism turned on Communism as well as on Christianity; its greatest fury, however, was directed with demoniac instinctiveness against the original protagonist of the concept of Oneness as the fundamental value and the basic ideal—against the Jew.

Looking at the contemporary scene, the Jew is astounded by the uncanny stagecraft of the mysterious producer: the unifying genius of a Jew, exiled from his home by the dark rebellion against unity, placing in the hands of the colossi the power that may destroy all in the conflict of the two ideologies that each have its root in its own variation of the Judaic theme of Oneness. Does the solution lie, as Toynbee suggests, not in one prevailing over the other, but in transcending both ideologies by a new vision and a new way of life? In terms of Judaism this could only mean the transcending of the materialistic, this-worldly Kingdom of Man as well as that of the spiritual, other-worldly Kingdom of God: the interpenetration of the two by the Judaic transformation of this world into the Kingdom of God. In the building of this world as a Kingdom of God, the power of physical nature would become the benevolent helpmate of man in the sanctification of the Mundane by readying it to receive the imprint of a purpose from on high.

Most baffling of all, however, is the unique phenomenon that, at this Zero Hour of mankind, the old-new people of the Jews, having proved by its survival that man may overcome all odds against him, is returning to its ancient homeland, as it has always proclaimed that one day it would. Once again it may take up the long-interrupted task of working in its homeland for the establishment of "this World" as God's Kingdom.

Pondering over such an extraordinary constellation of issues and events, the Jew remembers the opinion of a Christian historian, who once called Judaism the Ferment of History.[26] Perhaps the Word of the Living God on this subject has not yet been heard or, if heard, not yet understood. In the meantime, let Jewry continue its path through history, serving God as it has been given to it to understand Him and His service; striving and working, praying and hoping, living and—if need be —suffering for the transformation of this Kingdom of Man into the Kingdom of God; firm in the faith that the words of the prophet will not fail to be fulfilled:

In that day shall there be upon the bells of the horses: Holy Unto the Lord . . . Yea, every pot in Jerusalem and in Judah shall be holy unto the Lord of hosts.[27]

147

NOTES

CHAPTER I

1. VII/446-47.
2. *A Study of History* is actually completed with Volume IX; Volume X might appropriately be considered an annex to the rest of the work.
3. The quotations are taken from II/50 and 386-87.
4. I Kings, III/5 and 9.
5. II/55.
6. IV/68.
7. III/187.
8. VIII/467.
9. This meaning of "the retort" is taken from various passages in the *Study*, in particular from V/433, VII/228 and 424, I/293, VIII/472, V/120.
10. According to Mr. Toynbee's terminology, meaning the Roman Empire, which is to be considered the Universal State of the disintegrating Hellenic Civilization.
11. VI/302.
12. III/141.
13. V/68, footnote 2.
14. IV/225.
15. V/657-58.
16. IV/246.
17. See Josephus, *Antiquities of the Jews*, XIII/9.
18. V/657-58.
19. E.g., V/125-6, VIII/479, 446.
20. VII/73.
21. IV/228-29.
22. VI/260-61.
23. IV/225.
24. V/387.
25. See Josephus, *Antiquities of the Jews*, XIII/9.
26. There are historians who maintain that Constantine the Great, when making Christianity the state religion of the Roman Empire, was moved mainly by considerations of political expediency. While Mr. Toynbee, for reasons of his "psychological" penetration of the mentality of Constantine, rejects such a view (see V/708-10), he cannot help conceding (see IV/349-50) that the triumph of Christianity over the Empire was due to "promptings of Superstition . . . supported by the counsels of raison d'état." In order to preserve "the ancient unity of religious and political life in the Hellenic universal state . . . the bold diplomatic counterstroke was executed of taking the Christian Church bodily to the Empire's bosom". After the *entente* between Constantine and the Church, the latter—according to Mr. Toynbee—"nestled down promptly and cheerfully into the *political* shell in which the Imperial authorities now invited it to take up its abode . . ." Since "the bold diplomatic counterstroke" included the forcible suppression of all other religions besides Christianity (Judaism being the only one that was granted a very narrowly circumscribed measure of toleration), it would be interesting to know whether the establishment of Christianity by Constantine should be called "a policy of religious conversion by political force" or, perhaps, a policy of political unification by means of enforced religious uniformity? See also what Toynbee has to say (VII/401) about Theodosius I's new policy of repression against all non-Christian religion in 382 C.E., as a

NOTES

means for saving the Empire from dissolution. Be that as it may, it is interesting to note that the same deed that cost Judaism "the whole of its spiritual future," when performed on a world-wide scale, should have established the good fortune of Christianity. At the same time one cannot help recalling that another Christian scholar contemporary of Mr. Toynbee, John MacMurray, in his *The Key to History*, subjects the *entente* between Constantine and the Church to a criticism which is very similar to the one meted out to the Hasmonean Prince by Mr. Toynbee. MacMurray recognizes in this *entente* between Church and State the main cause for Christianity's failure in Western history.

27. V/175.
28. See above, sect. 1 of this chapter.
29. V/126, footnote 5.
30. V/126-27.
31. One of the charms of the *Study* is that it prevents Jews as well as Judaism from falling into the sin of vain conceit by imagining that there could be anything unique about either of them. In good and bad fortune, in their greatness as well as in their fall, they have for their yoke-fellows of destiny the Parsees and Zoroastrianism.
32. V/434.
33. V/387.
34. V/383.
35. V/387.
36. V/394.
37. IV/262-63.
38. IV/246.
39. See, e.g., IX/635.
40. X/3.
41. Quoted in *The Foot of Pride* by Malcolm Hay, Beacon Press, Boston, 1950.
42. II/286.
43. V/126.
44. VI/120; see also footnote.
45. VI/122, footnote 3. A fuller explanation of this point one finds in VI/130, footnote 3.
46. VI/121, footnote 2.
47. VI/123. It is good to have this reassurance. Otherwise one might have been inclined to believe that the Jewish aspiration for world dominion, unveiled by Mr. Toynbee, was the original form of the international Jewish conspiracy, which is the theme of the spurious *Protocol of the Elders of Zion.* Toynbee does not seem to consider the *Protocol* genuine; the Jewish hopes for world dominion were "finally extinguished, in the blood of the followers of Bar Kokaba" in the second century C.E.
48. VI/124-26.
49. IV/224 and III/141.
50. III/141.
51. VI/30.
52. VI/34-35. There is, of course, a problem posed by such an interpretation. There were other peoples beside the Jews who "shaped their conceptions of an Almighty God in the image of the Great King of a universal state." Why then did "the god of the Achaemenian emperors' insignificant Jewish subjects" become "the vehicle" for the revelation of the One True God to all mankind? Mr. Toynbee is especially perturbed by the fact that the tribal Jewish deity is provincial at home, impudent in exile, and altogether intolerant and jealous. The qualifications of "a barbaric and provincial Yahweh" would seem to be "so conspicuously inferior to those of so many of his unsuccessful competitors." See VI/39-41. Mr. Toynbee believes that two of its qualities were responsible for the victory of the uncouth deity of the

Jews. The Jews imagined their tribal god to be alive. It so happens that "God's essence" for Man is "that He is a living god with whom a living human being can enter into a spiritual relation." It is the most difficult divine attribute to discover and to grasp; only Jews were able to see and to equip with it their national divinity. Secondly, the very easy-going tolerance of the other divinities towards their competitors was their undoing. They were not ambitious enough; whereas the vulgar "devouring jealousness" of the Jewish god kept it in the race for "a monopoly of divinity." He who pushes hardest gets farthest. But not even Mr. Toynbee can miss the fact that mankind has failed to grasp the unity of God "in a world in which the God of Israel has not been on the scene," which seems to indicate that there may be something more in being nasty than "Sheer survival-value in a struggle for existence between competing divinities." "Its transcendent value lies in the disconcerting fact that a divinity who is credited by his worshippers with this spirit of uncompromising self-assertion proves to be the only medium through which the profound and therefore elusive truth of the unity of God has been firmly grasped hitherto by human souls." (See VI/49.) This is indeed disconcerting. There must be something wrong with the human soul or with the unity of God or—perhaps—with Mr. Toynbee himself, who may not know what he is talking about. His idea of devouring provincial jealousy as the receptacle for the concept of a Universal Omnipotent and True God is childish. He does put his finger on something important when he mentions the divine quality of Being-alive. However, he does not seem to be surprised that the most hidden attribute of God, the most difficult to grasp, should have been understood by primitive Israelites alone and in relationship to a rather "barbarous" concept of a local divinity. Be that as it may—and we shall yet deal more fully with the qualities of Being-alive and Jealousness (see below)—one cannot help being somewhat amused by what has developed for Mr. Toynbee in relationship to his *Study*. One of its basic principles indicates that there is nothing unique about either Judaism or Jewry, as there is nothing unique about anything else in human history. Everything happens in accordance with the general "pattern" and the "laws" which Mr. Toynbee uncovers with such ingenuity. But now he himself is compelled to concede that both the priceless treasure of a living Deity, without which religion in the Christian-Islamic-Judaic sense is inconceivable, and that "disconcerting" gadget of "a jealous god," without which—as a matter of fact—the unity of God has never been grasped by human souls, have been lifted into the light of history by some semi-barbarous Israelites; and not even Mr. Toynbee can formulate a "law" to account for it. Here, at last, is something without parallel, something outside the natural course of events, the one and only exception of all history. And what a fateful irregularity! Since in Mr. Toynbee's own opinion "Religion is the true end of man" (see VII/448) one cannot escape the conclusion that the entire purposeful destiny of the human race was entrusted into the hands of Israel. Lucky devil of an uncouth little parochial divinity, to have drawn the First (and only) Prize in the world's history, where otherwise—on the testimony of Mr. Toynbee—there are no lotteries and nothing is left to chance!

53. VI/124-6.
54. Ibid.
55. Ibid.
56. Ibid., 128.
57. See above p. 3 and V/433.
58. See above p. 12 and IV/262. Toynbee does say (see VI/101) that at times Futurism is "allowed to transcend itself through rising into Transfiguration." It remains however unexplained that, whereas in Vol. V Jewry finds God through a form of Transfiguration and loses Him later through Maccabean

Futurism, in Vol. VI Jewry is led to God via Futurism, which ultimately transcends itself in Transfiguration. It is impossible for both these versions to be true.

59. VI/46.
60. VI/268-69 and footnotes; also, ibid. 163 and footnote.
61. VI/458, 460.
62. II/73 and V/658.
63. Composed of VI/7 and 9; VII/511 and IX/623; VI/125. Far be it from us to argue with the distinguished Christian scholar about the source of the "human inspiration in Jesus." If he asks us to believe that Jesus had no knowledge of Isaiah, Micah, Jeremiah, the Psalms, and a great body of the Jewish teaching of his time, containing innumerable variations on the Mosaic theme of "God of the spirits of all flesh," we must assume that he has valid reason for doing so. It is, however, rather confusing that in Vol. VI it is the Alexandrine discovery of the brotherhood of men (or, since Alexander himself, like Ikhnaton about ten centuries before him, perhaps "learnt the mystery from the lips of Amon's priests" [see VI/247, footnote] the Alexandrine vision of it), presupposing the fatherhood of God, that inspired Jesus; whereas in other places (e.g., IX/623) we are told that the brotherhood of men was "an original Christian belief . . . and this Christian belief . . . was a corollary of a Christian discovery—or revelation—of the fatherhood of God." Toynbee seems to be no less uncertain about Christianity than he is about Judaism.
64. V/658.
65. VI/537.
66. See above p. 11 and V/126.
67. See above p. 6.
68. It should be Aristobolus, who—having conquered the Itureans of a frontier district in North Galilee—converted them to Judaism. See Josephus, *Antiquities of the Jews*, XIII/11.
69. VIII/279, footnote.
70. See above p. 8-9 and V/175.
71. V/175 and 126-27; and 126, footnote 5.
72. See above p. 11.
73. If it were not so depressing to witness in this "mid-twentieth Christian century" so much literary ingenuity spent on such an unworthy cause, one could only be amused by the way the true nature of the Toynbean reasoning does break through the camouflage of ambiguity. Having declared that the Maccabean temper or Maccabeanism, as "a vein in the Christian religion," recoiled upon Jewry in anti-Semitism, Mr. Toynbee—as we saw—hastened to add that "Maccabeanism" (i.e., the Maccabean temper) was not the sole reason. But a "fanatical religious intolerance" combined with a socially and economically conditioned antipathy to become an "aggravation" of an already existent anti-Semitism. But it was—and this is the "tragic irony"—by the Judaic element in its ethos that Christianity was betrayed. Since, however, a "fanatical religious intolerance" is the same as "Maccabeanism" or the Maccabean temper, which, having been inherited by Christendom, became "this Jewish vein in the Christian religion"; and since the "Judaic element" in the Christian ethos is identical with "Maccabeanism" or with "a fanatical religious intolerance" or the Maccabean temper—then what Mr. Toynbee says about the tragic irony of Christian anti-Semitism may also be paraphrased in this manner: "Maccabeanism" is not the only reason for Christian anti-Semitism, but the combination of this Maccabean "vein in the Christian religion" with "an antipathy" was an aggravation of pre-Christian anti-Semitism into which Christianity was betrayed by the Maccabean, not the Hellenic, vein in its ethos. What Mr. Toynbee actually says is that "the aggravation," which was the result of the combination of the Maccabean vein in Christianity with

"an antipathy," was caused by the "Maccabean vein in Christianity." It is as logical as to say that it is because of A that A + B is C. It is, of course, nonsense; but it is the acme of Mr. Toynbee's ingenious method of holding on to contradictory interpretations of Judaism. At first, with the help of the Maccabean "ism," he smuggles the Maccabean temper into Christianity, as a "vein" in that religion, as a Judaic element in it. Having thus safely lodged the "Judaic element" in Christianity, he reverts to the proper literary and logical difference between a "temper" in people and an "element" in a religion. To enhance ambiguity, he replaces "the Maccabean temper" (alias Maccabean "vein," alias "Judaic element") by a "fanatical religious intolerance"; and thus the statement that the "Judaic element" (alias Maccabean "vein," alias Maccabean temper) was responsible for the combination of "a fanatical religious intolerance" with "an antipathy" can be made to sound plausible.

74. VII/438, footnote 2.
75. Ibid., 431.
76. Ibid., 474, footnote 1, and VIII/406.

CHAPTER II

1. Isaiah 45/1.
2. Our italics.
3. See above p. 21 the censure of escapism and VI/127.
4. VI/130, footnote 3. Toynbee identifies the "Lord's Anointed" with the Messiah. But nowhere in the Jewish Bible does the term have the meaning of "Redeemer." It is always priests and Kings of Judah and Israel that are meant; the anointed ones alone are consecrated for office. In the Psalms (see 105/15), the term occurs in the plural. The only exception is, perhaps the mysterious passage in Daniel 9/25, where the use of the term is not at all clear. At the same time, the "Lord's Anointed" is not found anywhere in the Messianic passages of the Jewish Bible. The term Messiah, does derive from the Hebrew for the "Lord's Anointed"; it does mean "the anointed one." But it received its specific technical significance of "Redeemer" in post-Biblical times. See, e.g., *Hasting's Encyclopedia of Religion and Ethics*. The "Lord's Anointed" in connection with Cyrus indicates that the authority of Cyrus' kingship is to be considered as if he had been consecrated for office; he is king by the Grace of God. That such dignity is conceded to a Gentile is in itself a manifestation of the prophet's universalism and in keeping with the other, more significant, aspects of his teaching.
5. Ibid., 155.
6. These concepts are, as anyone fairly familiar with the Bible of Israel may recall, no original discoveries of "Deutero-Isaiah." There are innumerable parallel passages in the books of Moses and of the Prophets, as well as in the other Writings. It is true that the Universal Creator and Savior is also referred to as "the God of Israel"; the phrase has been the stumbling block of Christian theologians through the ages. The context, in which they occur, proves, as in the case of "Deutero-Isaiah," that no tribal deity is meant. proves, as is in the case of "Deutero-Isaiah," that no tribal deity is meant The "God of Israel" does not mean of Israel alone. See below ch. III, sect. 2 for a Jewish interpretation of the term.
7. Isaiah X/5.
8. Ibid., LIII.
9. VI/277-78.
10. Josephus, *Antiquities of the Jews*, XII/7-3.
11. Ibid., XVIII/1-6.
12. Dio Cassius, *Roman History*, LXIX, 12; quoted by Dubnow, *Weltgeschichte des Jüd. Volkes*, III/55.

13. Josephus gives us a vivid description of the last of the Roman procurators, Gessius Florus (64-66): ". . . Gessius Florus, as though he had been sent on purpose to show his crimes to everybody, made a pompous ostentation of them to our nation, as never omitting any sort of violence, nor any unjust sort of punishment; for he was not moved by pity and never was satisfied with any degree of gain that came in his way; nor had he any more regard to great than to small acquisitions, but became a partner with the robbers themselves. For a great many fell then into that practice without fear, as having him for their security, and depending on him, that he would save them harmless in their particular robberies . . ." *Antiquities,* XX/11-1. Of Antonius Felix, a predecessor of Florus by four years (52-60), Tacitus says in his *History* (V/8-9): ". . . Antonius Felix, indulging in every kind of barbarity and lust, exercised the power of a king in the spirit of a slave." At the end of his remarks about Felix, Tacitus continues with the significant statement: "Yet the *endurance* of the Jews lasted till Gessius Florus was procurator. In his time the war broke out." In order to appreciate the kind of objectivity that distinguishes the historian Toynbee one has to compare what he has to say about the conduct of Rome in Judea with this testimony of the Roman historian, who—as is well known—was far from partial to the Jews. Whereas Tacitus acknowledges the vileness of the Roman provocation and recognizes the high degree of Jewish endurance and restraint, in a number of passages Mr. Toynbee is quite annoyed with the noble Romans who showed so much moderation towards the Jews (e.g., VI/201) and maintains that "the Romans, in their dealings with the Jews, exercised almost *super-human self-restraint* before the Zealots forced their hand . . ." in 66 C.E. and finally in 132. (VII/112) Tacitus is of course not unknown to Mr. Toynbee, but his testimony must be ignored for it provides no confirmation whatever for "the satanic emeute of the Jewish Zealots."

14. VII/314-15. The reference is to the following passage from Suetonius. *The Lives of the Twelve Caesars* (quoted here after the Modern Library edition, p. 335): "When Titus found fault with him for contriving a tax upon public toilets, he held a piece of money from the first payment to his son's nose, asking whether its odor was offensive to him. When Titus said 'No,' he replied, 'Yet it comes from urine'." Mr. Toynbee obviously has a delicate sense of humor, for which the late Julius Streicher, gauleiter of Bavaria and editor of the *Stuermer* might well have envied him. Strangely enough, his sense of humor deserts him when, only a few pages further on (ibid., 339), he describes the same kind of "Jewish" attitude adopted by the primitive Christians toward the worship of Caesar. They refused to serve in the Roman army, though not for long, because they objected, among other things, to "the worship of the Emperor's genius and offer of sacrifice to it, and the veneration of military standards as idols." One wonders what the primitive Christians used for money: or, since they did not school themselves to *seeing, handling, using, earning, hoarding* it—which, as is well known only Jews would do—did they perhaps overlook the fact that the image, as abominable to them as to the Jews, was on Caesar's coin?

15. The essay is found in Gregorovius' *Wanderjahre in Italien;* it was written in 1853. An English translation of the essay alone was published by Schocken Books, New York, in 1948. Our quotation is from that edition, page 31; italics ours.

16. V/648 and VI/201-02.

17. Even Toynbee cannot help acknowledging this, at least by implication, when (in a footnote, VI/181-2,3) he mentions Philo's magnificent tribute to Augustus. There he says: "Yet this Jewish enthusiast for Augustus and his work would have rejected as a shocking blasphemy any suggestion that he should express his gratitude towards a human saviour by paying him those

divine honours that, in Philo's belief, were payable exclusively to the One True God."

18. Henry VIII of England was of course much more representative of Christianity than the Hasmonean princes, under discussion, were of Judaism. The Tudor king did establish a specific branch of the Church in Christendom, whereas Hyrcanus, Aristobolus, and Alexander Jannai were without any influence on Judaism.

19. VI/122, footnote 2.

20. VII/341.

21. See, e.g., I/288, footnote 3; V/78 and 382.

22. Zechariah, VIII/16.

23. According to another version: ". . . but like servants who minister to their master on condition of receiving no reward." The consistency of the Jewish ethos on this point is nobly illustrated by the Hassidic anecdote concerning the saintly Dov Baer of Mezritch. In his early years, the Maggid lived in great poverty with his young wife. When their child was born, he did not have the penny for which the midwife asked in order to buy some camomile tea for the baby. In his sorrow, out of pity for his child, the Maggid gave a sigh, whereupon he heard a voice say to him: "You have lost your share in the Coming World." In his answer the Maggid exclaimed: ". . . . the reward has been done away with. Now I can begin to serve in good earnest." See Martin Buber, *Tales of the Hasidim, Early Masters,* pp. 98-99. Schocken Books, New York, 1945.

24. See Josephus, *Antiquities of the Jews,* XIV/9-4, XV/1-1 and 10-4.

25. V/75, italics ours.

26. Aboth de Rabbi Nathan, VI/5.

27. Talmud Yerushalmi Nedarim, V/6.

28. Talmud Babli, Succah, 28.

29. In fact, the Talmudic source quotes Rabbi Johanan ben Zakkai in fuller explanation of the phrase used by Simon the Just. The idea that "lovingkindness" was greater than sacrifice had been taught by the Pharisees—following the prophetic tradition—before Rabbi Johanan ben Zakkai. Rabbi Johanan ben Zakkai, being a contemporary of the fall of Jerusalem, was the first to use it as a thought of comfort at a moment of despair. On this point see, e.g., Leo Baeck, *The Pharisees and Other Essays,* Schocken, New York.

30. VIII/580.

31. IX/521.

32. Isaiah, XXX/15.

33. Zechariah, IV/6.

34. IV/650 and footnote 1 ibid.

35. Jeremiah, I/9-10.

36. Isaiah, XI.

37. The "transfiguration" of the military metaphor, far from being a Pauline discovery, is the routine Pharisaic method of the Midrash and Talmud to interpret many of the Biblical references to war.

38. VI/178-180.

39. *Ethics of the Fathers,* II/7. There our quotation is found among some sayings by Hillel the Younger. Language, style, and contents, however, indicate that its proper place is in the first chapter of the *Ethics,* among the sayings attributed to Hillel the Older. In Talmud Babli, tractate Succah, 53/a, the statement is clearly attributed to Hillel the Older.

40. VII/339.

41. The only possible comparison between the primitive Christians and the Jews could be with Jewry in its Babylonian Exile, which according to Toynbee found its final "enlightenment" in the weeping by the waters of Babylon and almost accomplished for the Neo-Babylonian Empire what Christianity did

in the arena of the Romano-Hellenic universal state. See V/120-2; VII/163 and 228; and above p. 3-4.

42. IV/226-27.
43. VIII/314.
44. In view of Gandhi's Satyagraha and its awe-inspiring implementation against an oppressive imperial power, we are prepared to limit the validity of this statement to the arena of—to use a Toynbean phrase—the Judaic religions, i.e., Christianity, Islam, and Judaism; though in Toynbee's philosophy the "Non-Violence of Jesus and Johanan ben Zakkai" are of a higher spiritual quality than that of Gandhi. See V/588-89.
45. VII/450.
46. VII/453 and 506.
47. VII/545.
48. VII/556.
49. Ibid., 563.

CHAPTER III

1. VII/439.
2. See Matt. III/7-12, ibid., XIII/41-42; Hebrews X/31, ibid., XII/29; Luke XII/5; Romans, I/18, ibid., IX/22; I Thessalonians I/7-8; Revelation XIV/10. An objective analysis of the fulmination of Jesus against the Pharisees one may find in *The Pharisees* by R. Travers Herford. For a comparison between the Toynbean and a sounder Christian position on the subject of the Wrath of God one may consult *Symbolism and Belief* by Edwyn Bevan. A summary criticism of Toynbee's point of view is found in an annex to Vol. VII of his *Study* by Martin Wight under the heading: "The Crux for an Historian Brought Up in the Christian Tradition," pp. 737-48.
3. VII/718.
4. Exodus XXXIV/6. The Authorized Version has "goodness" instead of "loving-kindness." The Hebrew *Hesed* is better rendered however with "love and kindness."
5. See Deuteronomy VI/5 and Leviticus XIX/18 and 33. Also Matt. XXII/40.
6. IX/401.
7. VII/725 and IX/382.
8. Exodus III/14.
9. Sh'moth Rabba, III/6.
10. See the analysis of the *Mysterium Tremendum* by Rudolph Otto in his book *Das Heilige.*
11. Genesis XVIII/25-27.
12. Psalms, 103/13. The Hebrew word, which is here translated as "compassion" (*Holy Scriptures, A New Translation,* London and Philadelphia, the Jewish Publication Society of America), is the same as used in the phrase "Father of Mercy." See also *Talmud Babli,* Berahot 35/B. "A man's father is none but the Holy One, blessed be He."
13. Deuteronomy XXXII/6. Cf. also Malachi I/6: "If then I be a father, where is My honor? And if I be a master, where is My fear?"
14. Talmud Babli, Ta'anith, 25/B; quoted after the text of the Ain Yaakob editions.
15. Talmud Babli, Megillah 31/A. Quoted after the translation of the Authorized Daily Prayer Book, by the Rev. S. Singer, London.
16. Psalms VIII/5-6.
17. Ethics of the Fathers, III/18.
18. Aboth de' Rabbi Nathan, II/5.
19. Psalms XIX/8-11.

20. See, for example, Talmud Babli, Menahot, 43/B. "Our Teachers have taught: Beloved is Israel, for the Holy One blessed be He, surrounded them with commandments."

21. Talmud Babli, Pesahim, 87/B. Obviously suggested by Habbakuk, III/2, "In wrath remember compassion," even though not quoted.

22. Isaiah XIX/24-25.

23. Talmud Babli, Sanhedrin, 37/A, Mishnah.

24. Malachi, II/10.

25. That the idea of a Peculiar People does not necessarily clash with that of a Universal God of all humanity is also exemplified by the saying attributed to Alexander, the Great, (quoted by Toynbee, VI/9), who maintained: "God is the common father of all men, but he makes the best ones peculiarly his own." Toynbee, a great admirer of Alexander, weighs the possibility that the Hellenic conqueror might have been influenced by the priests of Amon-Ra. See above page — and VI/247, footnote; the saying, which he quotes according to Plutarch, however, has a typically "Jewish" ring about it.

26. Deuteronomy, XIV/2.

27. Hermann Cohen rightly points out that the covenant with Abraham is preceded by the covenant with Noah, which is "the everlasting covenant between God and every living creature of all flesh that is upon the earth." See "Die Religion der Vernunft, etc.," Leipzig, 1919, p. 137 and 386.

28. Exodus, IV/22.

29. Quoted by Edwyn Bevan, *Symbolism and Belief*, p. 290.

30. Malachi, II/6.

31. As we saw, above, p. 150n, VI/42, Toynbee himself recognized that the concept of a "Living" God was unique to Israel and without it mankind would not have been able to reach the One True God. What he does not see is that the "Living" God is not the Philosopher's God just because He is not found in abstract thinking and reveals Himself only in "history." If Jews knew about Him, it was because they actually encountered Him. To associate the "Living" God, as Toynbee does, with a tribal deity, shows that even though one might have read a great deal about theology, it is still possible not to have grasped the basic element in the religious encounter.

32. Deuteronomy, IX/6, and Amos III/2.

33. Talmud, Gerim, I/7. See also Talmud Babli, Yebamot, 24/B.

34. See Talmud Babli, Ketubot, 11/A.

35. See Talmud, Gerim, IV/3, Midrash Rabba, Bamidbar, VIII/2 and 9.

36. Galatians, III/28. For Toynbee see VIII/626.

37. Midrash Rabba, Sh'moth, XIX/4.

38. Ibid., Bamidbar, VIII/9.

39. Talmud Babli, Baba Kama, 38/A. See also Safra on Leviticus, XVIII/5, where Rabbi Jeremiah says the same, but basing it on a rich selection of textual support. That he repeats the saying of Rabbi Meir literally but without mentioning his name indicates that the saying as such was widely known among the Pharisees.

40. The most comprehensive form of religious universalism one finds in the Midrashic Tanna debey Eliyahu Rabba, Ch. 10, where it is said: ". . . whether Jew or Gentile, man or woman, male or female slave, the holy spirit rests on them in accordance with their deeds."

41. The formulation of Maimonides, based on Talmud Babli, Sanhedrin, 105/A; Tosefta Sanhedrin, XIII/2. See Maimonides, Yad HaHazakah, T'shubah, III/5; Eduth XI/10; Mlahim VIII/11.

42. Tanna Debey Eliyahu Zuta, XX.

43. Galatians, III/26.

44. John, XIV/6.

45. VII/428, footnote 2. See there and p. 442; also the annexes ibid.: *Religions*

and Psychological Types; and also: *The Crux for a Christian Historian,*
by M. Wight.

46. Malachi, I/11.
47. Psalms, XXIX. This is the literal meaning of the Hebrew original, which
—of course—differs somewhat from its literary rendering in English trans-
lations of the Bible.
48. Midrash Rabba, Exodus, V/9. The concluding sentence, "Said the Holy One
etc. . . ." is found ibid. IX/I. Its original form the idea, probably, received
in the context in which it occurs, ibid., XXXIV/1.
49. VII/442.
50. An interesting illustration of this point one may find in Toynbee's own interpretation of the Communist ideology. Following loyally his own fabrica-
tion of the Judaic ethos of violence, as manifested in the historically non-
existent "Maccabean Judaism," Mr. Toynbee says that "the distinctively
Jewish element" in Communism is the "apocalyptic vision of a violent revolution" which is to bring about the elevation of Communism's "Chosen
People," the Proletariat, to sole dominion in the "Kingdom of This World."
On the other hand, "the distinctively Christian element" in the Communist
inspiration is "an Ecumenicalism which is positively antipathetic, and not
merely foreign, to the Jewish tradition." Jesus' injunction, "Go ye into all
the world and preach the Gospel to every creature," was taken over by Marx
and his followers. "It is not merely a revolution but a world revolution that
the Good Marxian is in duty bound to strive for." (V/178-9). But it is
exactly its "Ecumenicalism" that makes Communism a threat to the rest of
the world and not its "Chosen People" concept. "Socialism in One Country"
may be acceptable to the rest of mankind; the Marxian World Revolution is
the real danger. There may indeed be an intrinsic relationship between
Christian and Marxian "Ecumenicalism" as Toynbee insists. Both are "har-
bingers of good tiding" for all mankind; both want to save all humanity
and both maintain that it alone possesses the secret of salvation. The Christian Kingdom is not of this World and no one can enter it but by faith in
"Christ Jesus"; the Communist Kingdom is this World but no one is admitted except by faith in "Dialectical Materialism." Christian "Ecumenicalism" is otherworldly religious totalitarianism; Marxian "Ecumenicalism" is
this-worldly secular totalitarianism. It is quite correct that this type of
"Ecumenicalism . . . is positively antipathetic, and not merely foreign, to
the Jewish tradition."

It is part of Toynbee's assertions that in the apocalyptic writings the
"Jewish way of Violence" found literary expression and it was not until the
establishment of a new Jewry by Rabbi Johanan ben Zakkai that these writings were "ejected from the canon of the Law and the Prophets." See V/76.
No less fantastic than the idea of the founding of a new Jewish ethos by
Rabbi Johanan ben Zakkai, with which we have dealt above, is the suggestion concerning the "Judaic" apocalyptic vision of Violence. The apocalypse
was the product of the feverish fantasy of some Jews, living in a time of
crisis and violence. The apocalyptic writings were never "ejected from the
canon of the Law and the Prophets" because, for very good reason, they
were never admitted into the canon of Judaism. Strangely enough "apocalyptic visions of violent revolution" figure much more prominently in the New
Testament than in the Jewish Bible, and Christianity, to this day, has been
much more preoccupied with them than Judaism. Similarly significant is the
case of the books of the Maccabees. They were never part of the Jewish
Bible; Judaism ignored them completely; but they have received considerable
attention from the Christian Church. In the records of authentic Judaism, in
Midrash and Talmud, very little mention is made of the Maccabees and no
significance at all is attached to their military prowess.

51. *The Inferno,* Canto XX. A New Translation by John Ciardi, A Mentor Classic.
52. Quoted after *Symbolism and Belief,* by E. Bevan, p. 237.
53. Talmud Babli, Sanhedrin, 39/B. The same thought found a somewhat different formulation in a probably much older, anonymous Midrash. It is asked why the expression of rejoicing does not occur in the Bible in connection with the Passover festival, whereas it does occur several times in the description of the observance of the other two (Shabuoth and Succoth) festivals. And the answer is given: "Because the Egyptians died during Passover.... Similarly, you also find that on the occasion of Passover the 'Hallel' (the traditional festival hymn in praise of God) is said only the first night and the first day, but not the other six days as is customary during the seven days of the Succoth festival. Why so? Because it is said (Proverbs 24/17): 'Rejoice not when thine enemy falleth, and let not thy heart be glad when he stumbleth.' " See Yalkut Shimoni, on Leviticus, XXIII, 40. To this day, only "half-Hallel" is recited at the Passover services on the last six days of the festival. For another reason of this custom, however, see Talmud Babli, ERHIN, 10, A and B.
54. VII/463; also IV/262-3, on Jewry's "resting on their oars" in the conceit of a "privileged" people.
55. See Matt. XV/24. "But he answered and said, I am not sent but unto the lost sheep of the house of Israel."
56. See above Chapter III, section 2.
57. VIII/574 and 576.
58. See, e.g., VII/550, 556.
59. See *Physics and Philosophy,* by Sir James Jeans, Cambridge University Press, p. 183.
60. V/160.
61. See J. A. Hadfield, *Psychology and Morals,* N. Y., 1926.
62. VIII/283. The question is the more justified since Mohammedanism is—in Toynbee's opinion—a form of relapse into Judaism.
63. This consistent inclination of his to revive every one of the lowest prejudices and superstitions of the medieval Christian marketplace against Jewry and Judaism in the dishonestly expropriated garb of scholarly objectivity makes Mr. Toynbee a much more objectionable person than the honest anti-Semite, who does not falsify history in order to reject Judaism and Jewry.
64. VIII/283.
65. Quoted from *The Foot of Pride,* by Malcolm Hay, Beacon Press, Boston, 1950; page 30.
66. VII/560-2.
67. VIII/564.
68. See Plato, Gorgias; Steph. 472.
69. Isaiah, III/9.

CHAPTER IV

1. II/286. In the latter volumes of his work he is much less genial.
2. I/35 and ibid., 90.
3. II/55, footnote 4; ibid., 235, 402, and 405 footnote.
4. See the whole of Vol. VII.
5. See, e.g., IX/8.
6. *The Foot of Pride,* by Malcolm Hay, Beacon Press, Boston, 1950, p. 28.
7. VIII/599.
8. See, e.g., *Jewish Contributions to Civilization,* by Joseph Jacobs, The Jewish Publication Society of America, 1944; and *The Jewish Contribution to Civilization,* by Cecil Roth, East and West Library, London.
9. II/24, footnote 2.

NOTES

11. Cecil Roth, *The Jewish Contribution to Civilization*, East and West Library, London, pp. 35-7.
12. Ibid., 288-9. It is a coincidence that the reference to Julian is also made by Toynbee, who quotes the passage from the Emperor's letter extensively but with the intention of applying it to the "Early Christians." See Vol. V, p. 584. In that weird annex, Toynbee claims credit for whatever good there may be in Communism on behalf of early Christianity. He can do so by expropriating the social principles and ethics of the Jewish Essenes, from whose ranks were recruited many of the early Judeo-Christians.
13. V/126.
14. VII/493.
15. IX/167.
16. IX/382.
17. Deuteronomy, XXX/15-19.
18. Romans, VII/19.
19. See above Ch. I, sections 1 and 2.
20. VI/167.
21. Jeremiah, IX/22.
22. Bereshit Rabba, XXXV/3, the interpretation of Rabbi Aha, in the name of Rabbi Tanhum, the son of Rabbi Hiya; see also Maimonides, Moreh Nebuhim, Part III/54.
23. VIII/309.
24. See VI/64, VIII/533-4, ibid., 287, 291-301.
25. VIII/258-9.
26. II/252-54. It is noteworthy that a vestige of Toynbee's earlier and fairer position to the conflict in Palestine may still be found even in Volume VIII of his work. Discussing the havoc wrought in the East by that foreign intruder, Western nationalism, he points ot the divisions of India and of Palestine. See VIII/539. No doubt the Western ideology of nationalism had "a destructively explosive effect" in the East; however, as in India so in Palestine, its destructiveness was not due to a Zionist monopoly of nationalism.
27. VIII/289.
28. V/337. "This animal is very vicious; when one attacks it, it defends itself."
29. VIII/290.

CHAPTER V

1. V/394.
2. VI/149-157.
3. See, e.g., IX/621, 593, 444, 8, 573; VIII/273; VII/560-1; IX/555. There are also some passages where Toynbee attempts to leave man some share in his own salvation by making Transfiguration dependent on a kind of co-operation between God and Man.
4. VII/449.
5. Most revealing are Toynbee's vacillations on Rabbi Johanan ben Zakkai's role. At the close of the presentation of his "psychological" version of Judaism, he is very definite that the School of Rabbi Johanan ben Zakkai and the Christian Church differ in essentials from "mundane" Quietism and Zealotism alike. For the Rabbi and the Church "have ceased to set their heart upon the old mundane purpose of futurism and have put their treasure, instead, in a purpose which is not Man's but God's and which therefore can only be pursued in a spiritual field of supra-mundane dimensions." See VI/128 and above Ch. I, section 2. In an earlier volume, the Rabbi's ethos is described as being in the spirit of Jesus. See V/75-6, 390; but especially the Annex, ibid., 588, on the Ambiguity of Gentleness, where Toynbee differentiates between the non-violence of a quietist Agudath Israel, the tactical non-

NOTES

violence of Gandhi and the strategic non-violence of Jesus and Rabbi Johanan ben Zakkai. But in the latter part of the *Study* Toynbee reverses himself completely—as usual with him in such cases, without any further explanation—and identifies Rabbi Johanan with a specific manifestation of Zealotism. After the crushing defeat of the *militant* Zealots, says Toynbee, "the gentle vein of Jewish Zealotism came into its own at last when Rabbi Johanan ben Zakkai responded to the tremendous challenge of the fall of Jerusalem . . . by endowing Jewry with an inertly rigid institutional framework and a passively obstinate psychological habitus. . . ." See VIII/585. Far from acquainting Jews with the purposes of God, to be pursued "in a spiritual field of supra-mundane dimensions," he taught them Judaism as "a social drill"—see ibid. 599—for the sake of the purely mundane ambition of preserving Jewish communal identity in a politically impotent diaspora. Rabbi Johanan ben Zakkai could not have changed between Volumes V and VI and Volume VIII of the *Study;* but Toynbee has. As long as Transfiguration meant the transference of action from the Macrocosm to the Microcosm, the adoption of the ethos of gentleness—Toynbee's position in Volume V—it remained within the ken of men, and Rabbi Johanan ben Zakkai could also have been a protagonist of Transfiguration. Once, however, Transfiguration became an "otherworldly mystery," brought about by the direct action of God through the epiphany of Jesus and otherwise inaccessible for human beings—Toynbee's position in Volume VI—Rabbi Johanan could of course no longer be considered a "transfigurationist"; having been the key figure in Jewry after the fall of Jerusalem, he is turned into a "gentle Zealot," who is responsible for the preservation of a mundane Jewry. In Volume VI, which is the bridge in the Toynbean transformation, he is still permitted—not very logically, though—to have experienced Transfiguration, most probably because Toynbee himself, not fully realizing the consequences of his new theory, still clings to the "old" Rabbi of Volume V. It is an oversight, which is soon mended.

6. See, e.g., I/336; V/26; VI/279, footnote 6; VII/1.
7. I/53, 57, 165.
8. II/55. Italics ours; "the wandering of the nations" is a reference to the Heroic Ages of the external proletariat. See also V/658.
9. See, e.g., VII/6-7, 158, and the theme of Vol. III in general.
10. When once it was pointed out to Hegel that his philosophy was contradicted by facts, he answered: "All the worse for the facts." In the opinion of Toynbee, if Jewish survival contradicts his interpretation of history, all the worse for the Jews.
11. VIII/585, 599.
12. See, e.g., I/286, VI/275, VII/423-5. See also above Ch. I, section 1.
13. VI/216.
14. VI/123, footnote 5.
15. See Talmud Babli, Ketuboth, 110/B and 111/A and Maimonides, Mlahim, V/12.
16. VIII/601 and 576, footnote.
17. Ibid., 290.
18. Talmud Babli, Yebamoth, 121/B.
19. Ethics of the Fathers, II/5.
20. X/129.
21. See the concluding sentence in *Concerning Human Understanding,* by David Hume.
22. IX/433.
23. VIII/273.
24. *Our Inner Conflicts,* by Karen Horney, M.D., London, Routledge and Kegan Paul, p. 204.

25. Ibid., p. 120.
26. Ibid., 205.
27. Ibid., 204.
28. VIII/447.
29. See above, Ch. IV, section 1 and VI/216.
30. See above, Ch. IV, section 1 and IX/382-92.

CHAPTER VI

1. See, e.g., IV/6; also above Ch. IV, section 2.
2. The entire thesis of Toynbee that the internal proletariat of the Romano-Hellenic universal state produced the Christian universal church is questionable. Had Christianity never become the state religion of the Roman Empire by force of law, suppressing all other religions and grimly discriminating against Judaism, and had it yet succeeded in replacing all other competing religions, Toynbee would have a strong case. In view of the powerful mundane backing that Christianity received from Constantine the Great and men like the emperor Theodosius, one might perhaps be more justified in saying that it was the dominant minority of the Romano-Hellenic universal state that produced the Christian universal church. The distinguished historian Jacob Burckhardt has, for instance, this to say on the subject in his book *Force and Freedom,* (Meridian Books, New York, 1955, p. 123): "A new religion can arise beside the old one and divide the world with it, but can never oust it, even if it has conquered the masses, unless the state intervenes. . . . . All succumb to force if it is consistently applied, and especially if it is embodied in a single, inescapable world power like the Roman Empire. . . . Without the imperial legislation from Constantine to Theodosius, the Graeco-Roman religion would still be alive today." In another connection, the same author has this to say, (*ibid.,* 216): "Had it [Christianity] been left to itself, heresies and Gnostic sects might have destroyed it altogether. It was only the persecution which made the survival of *one* dominating central idea possible." See also above, Ch. I, note 26.
3. See above, Ch. II, section 3.
4. See, e.g., Talmud Babli, Ketuboth, 105/A and B.
5. Toynbee berates the author of the Ecloga for receiving his inspiration, in substituting mutilations for the death penalty, from the "correctly literal interpretation of the 'Lex Talionis' as enunciated in the Corpus Mosaicum." See IX/26. Neither he, nor the eighth-century Christian legislator, seems to have had the slightest inkling that long before the time of Jesus the Oral Law had so interpreted the "Lex Talionis" of the Mosaic Code that no punishments in the form of bodily mutilations were permitted, or ever executed, but payment of damages was substituted for them. See Talmud Babli, Baba Kama, 83/B. There are some other curious passages in the *Study*—see IX/88-95—about the "evocation of the Ghost of Judaism in Christianity." What is really being "evoked" is the ghost of the literal interpretation of the Mosaic Law, i.e., Sadduceeism. It would appear that in the course of history all kinds of Christian sects—and even the Church at one time or other—practiced "the meticulous observance of the Mosaic Law"; Jewry, on the other hand, thanks to the Pharisees, has never done it. Similarly, what Toynbee calls (IX/95) the Pharisaic "heartlessness of the legalistic observance" of the Sabbath is but a Christian fairy tale. The Pharisees, and again long before the time of Jesus, had fully acknowledged the precedence of life over Sabbath observance in case of a conflict between the two and therefore taught that where there was even only a *possible* danger to life not only was it permitted but commanded to break the law. Generations after the principle had been established, the Rabbis of the first half of the second century C.E. were attempting to discover a justifica-

161

tion of the practice in the "letter of the Law." It may be worth recording here that one of the Rabbis found the justification in the words of the Bible (*Exodus,* 31/14): ". . . . for it [the Sabbath] is holy unto you." "Unto you," he interpreted, means that the Sabbath is given over unto you but you are not given over unto the Sabbath. See, e.g., Talmud Babli, Yoma, 85/B. This, by the way, is a good illustration of how the Pharisees solved the problem of the "letter of the Law." The letter does not "kill" in their hands; it speaks for the Spirit, which is alive in the wholeness of the Torah and in the continuity of tradition and practices in a living Jewry; it is made to subserve life. Or as another Rabbi in the same context explains: "The Bible says (Leviticus, 18/5): 'Ye shall therefore keep My statutes, and Mine ordinances, which if a man do, he shall live by them . . .'; so that he shall *live* by them but not so that he shall die by them." The solution is not the same as that in the New Testament; but there is a solution because there is no rigidity and obstinacy. There is no meticulous observance of the "Mosaic Law" as Christians insist on believing; there is charity, but there is also law and discipline. On the Pharisees see the work of the Christian scholar, already mentioned, R. Travers Herford, *The Pharisees;* and the essays of Leo Baeck, *The Pharisees and Other Essays,* Schocken, New York.

6. See above Chapter II, section 3.
7. See Talmud Babli, Rosh Hashanah, 29/B, 30/B, 31/B.
8. Ethics of the Fathers, II/17. See also Talmud Babli, Sabbath 50/B and the conversation of Hillel with his disciples in Midrash Rabba, Vayikra, XXXIV/3, about bodily hygiene is an opportunity for Divine Service. The principle is comprehensively formulated by Maimonides in a well-known passage, Hilhot Deoth, III/2-3. The introductory words to the Tur, Orah Hayim, which is the first volume of the code that contains what Toynbee calls, "Judaism as a practice of social drill," read: "Be strong like the leopard, fast like the deer, and brave like the lion to do the Will of Thy Father in Heaven." The sentence is a quotation from the Talmud, Ethics of the Fathers, V/21.
9. VIII/474.
10. VII/522.
11. V/658.
12. VIII/511; IX/302.
13. VII/438.
14. In a somewhat ironic vein, Toynbee realizes that this might well have been Jewry's own justification for not exploiting the opportunities which eventually made the fortunes of Judaism's two daughter religions. See IX/87. He entertains the curious notion that Judaism, in its victory over Baal and Ashtoreth, did not escape the fate of all other victorious religions; for both of these divinities "slyly" crept back "into the fold of Jewish orthodoxy in the guise of personifications of the Lord's 'Word,' 'Wisdom,' and 'Angel.' " See IX/305 and VII/718. Toynbee does not have the slightest notion of the significance of the "Memra" ("Word," "Wisdom," and "Angel") for Judaism. The comparison with the God Incarnate in Christianity or the worship of the Kaaba in Islam is ridiculous. The "Memra" (or as it is also called, the Dibbur nivra, created speech), the personified Wisdom, or the Philonic concept of a supreme Angel-Logos, is not a principle of faith or a tenet of Judaism but a philosophical speculation. The overwhelming majority of the Jews, and especially of orthodox Jews, of all times, have lived and died without ever having heard of the idea. The average Jew, when he is told about it, finds the speculation queer and boring. This in itself should be sufficient to show that the "Memra" has nothing in common with "the repeatedly resurgent yearning for a God Incarnate" that "beset the Judaic

concept of the One True God's Transcendence" (i.e., in Christianity and Islam!). The "yearning" for a God Incarnate, for "personification," the relapse into polytheistic beliefs, is the yearning of the people, who are untrained in abstract thinking, for whom the One True God is much too aloof. The Logos or Memra in Judaism, mostly unknown to the people, belongs to the esoteric speculation of Jewish philosophers, whence it has found its way into the Kabbalah, the Jewish mystic lore. The specific Philonic interpretation of the concept was of very great influence on Christianity but was—significantly—ignored by Judaism. Other Jewish philosophers, e.g., Saadya (892-942 C.E.), conceived the "created Word" for the very opposite reason to the one presumed by Toynbee. The purpose was to make God still more "aloof" and transcendent. Biblical expressions like "God spoke," "God said," etc., appeared to Jewish philosophers much too anthropomorphic. In order to purify the idea of God of every trace of anthropomorphism, it was said that God did not speak Himself, which would indicate some form of "incarnation" and was therefore inconceivable and inadmissible, but created a Word to convey His message.

15. See above Chapter IV, section 1.
16. Talmud Eduyot, V/6.
17. How great an importance Toynbee attaches to this-worldly success of an otherworldly higher religion one may judge by his theory that the four living higher religions are the component parts of one great Heavenly Harmony, each of them being a specific variation on the same theme. See above p. —. Nowhere in the *Study* is any philosophical or theological reason given why the Harmony of Religions should have four, and not five or six or a dozen, components. Toynbee does attempt to discover a correspondence between the four psychological types of Jung and the four higher religions, Christianity, Islam, Mahayana, Hinduism. Each of the higher religions gives satisfaction to one of the four psychological types. (See, especially, the Annex on the subject in Vol. VII/717. The theory by itself is, of course, not to be taken seriously; though Toynbee does offer it in all seriousness. See, e.g., the criticism of Martin Wight, in the Annex, "The Crux for an Historian, etc.," ibid., 737). Reasoning on the assumption of the correctness of the premise, one is entitled to say that Judaism, having been the religion of Jewry for several thousands of years, must also have satisfied a psychological need. Whatever Jews be, whether there is any correspondence between them and any of the four "Jungian" types or not, they probably have some kind of a psyche with its needs. If then the criterion of being alive is the satisfaction of psychological needs, Judaism too ought to be one of the living higher religions. In actual fact Toynbee does not believe that each of the four religions has a specific message, which he accepts as valid for himself. No one can have four religions at the same time. He believes that whatever light there may be "in non-Christian systems of thought or conduct or worship is the work of Christ upon them and within them. By the Word of God—that is to say, by Jesus Christ—Isaiah and Plato and Zoroaster and the Buddha and Confucius conceived and uttered such truths as they declared." See VII/429. Should we then say that the three non-Christian higher religions are "living" on account of the few rays of Christian light that they incorporate? Surely then Judaism too must have some of it; e.g., Isaiah, the Psalms, the "two commandments" which Jesus declared to be the entire law. Be it the psychological or the theological criterion there is no justification for the exclusion of Judaism from the rank of the living higher religions. Nor does Toynbee attempt any such justification. His motivation is much simpler. Hinduism or Buddhism or Mohammedanism have hundreds of millions of followers; each of the three is the dominant religion of populous nations in broad regions of the World. It would be ridiculous to declare any

of the three "fossilized." It is different with a small people, of which the majority live in the Diaspora and which has never been very "successful."

18. See, e.g., VII/556.
19. See above p. —.
20. Quoted from *Shebet Mussar* in *Time and Eternity* by N. N. Glatzer, Schocken, New York.
21. See, e.g., VIII/447.
22. Ethics of the Fathers, III/21.
23. Jeremiah, IX/22-23; see above Chapter IV, section 1.
24. See VII/524, where Toynbee quotes the late Archbishop of Canterbury, Dr. William Temple, who recognizes the positive value of the promises of the Jewish Messianic Kingdom as expressed, e.g., in Isaiah IX/6-7 and XXV/6. But Dr. Temple adds: ". . . they have one fatal defect. They all represent ways of securing the outward obedience of men apart from inward loyalty; they are ways of controlling conduct, but not ways of controlling hearts and wills. . . ." This, too, is an opinion which is not based on the evidence offered by Judaism but prescribes what Judaism must be in order to justify age-old, pre-conceived ideas of Christianity. In many passages the prophets of Israel have made it clear that it is man's knowledge of God that will establish the Kingdom and that it is the Spirit of the Lord that moves the Messiah. In addition to the passage here quoted from Jeremiah, see Isaiah II/2-4; XI/1-9. How radically, the Pharisees, the successors to Israel's prophets, rejected any suggestion of "securing outward obedience apart from inward loyalty" one may appreciate from the following dictum: "Even a sin, when committed for its own sake, is more valuable than a divine commandment performed not for its own sake." See Talmud Babli, Berahot, 63/A. At the same time, one cannot help feeling that a spokesman of a civilization that has so singularly failed in both the control of external conduct and that of hearts and wills, as testified by Toynbee's own evaluation of the Western world, ought to show some signs of a healthy respect even for such a puny matter as the "control of external conduct." If one could only achieve that little thing, there would be much more on the credit and much less on the debit side of the Western account of history.
x. *Exodus*, XIX/6.
25. We do not deny the possibility of miracles. But when they happen, they are the results of direct divine intervention in the realm of human existence. According to Jewish teaching one must not plan one's life and face one's responsibilities counting on miracles. "We do not rely on miracles" is a saying of the Rabbis. Talmud Babli Pesahim, 64/A.
26. See, e.g., *Die Stellung des Menschen im Kosmos*, the fine essay by the modern German philosopher, Max Scheler. Scheler, however, assumes that his position is not compatible with a theistic philosophy.
27. VIII/498.
28. Midrash Rabba, Deuteronomy, II/22.
29. Isaiah, XI/9.
30. IX/346.
31. See I/9. This is how Toynbee defines "the spirit of Nationality." But nationality is neither a policy nor an ideology; it is a fact of life and history. Nations do exist. The spirit of nationality is a form of national self-awareness, which in itself is as little evil as is the self-awareness of the individual. To be oneself and to wish to remain oneself is not a form of egoism or even of egotism, but a healthy and natural manifestation of Life itself. What Toynbee actually defines would better be called the spirit of nationalism. Nationalism is a consciously conceived ideology of a nation's will to power, unimpeded by considerations of an ethical code of behavior towards others.

32. See Me'asef l'Tnuat he'Haluts, Warsaw, 1930.

CHAPTER VII

1. IX/412.
2. VII/63; VIII/87; IX/457.
3. See, e.g., VI/315-316.
4. VII/453, 506.
5. See, e.g., IX/426, where Toynbee's criticism of Gibbon contains a succinct summary of the moral debacle of the entire course of Western history, beginning with its earliest days.
6. IV/4; IX/412.
7. VI/314; IX/464.
8. IX/414.
9. IX/347, and 449.
10. IX/457-461.
11. IX/542.
12. IX/535.
13. IX/629, 628, 625.
14. VI/320, see Psalms 34/18; 51/17.
15. IX/630-1.
16. IX/635-7.
17. IX/528.
18. VIII/623-6.
19. It seems that at Zero Hour even the four living higher religions which Toynbee recognizes are of no avail. Islam, the Mahayana, and Hinduism are not even mentioned as possible sources of help. In Christian orthodoxy "the body of Christ . . . had been petrified into a pillar of salt." (IX/644) The universal churches seem to have reached the end of their journey. Left is the Crucifixion, the example of Jesus in the acceptance of suffering (somewhat anticipated by the "bodhisattva," see IX/632). Since Toynbee believes that Jesus is identical with the Godhead—see above Chapter I, section 3 and I/267-9 and notes—the epiphany of the Crucifixion can never be transcended.
20. Psalms, XLI/9. The rendering of Toynbee's final position, culled from IX/632, 634-5, 637, 644.
21. See V/189.
22. VI/260-1.
23. See VIII/480.
24. Ibid.
25. V/41.
26. Theodor Mommsen did, of course, not use the term in a sense flattering to the Jews. But how much better would it have been for Germany, as well as for the world at large, had the ferment of Judaism indeed succeeded in "decomposing" some parts of the German ethos.
27. Zechariah XIV/20-21.

INDEX

Aaron, 43
Aboth de Rabbi Nathan, 154, 155n
Abraham, the Patriarch, 68, 106, 156n
Adam, 64
Aelia Capitolina, 37
Africa, 78
    North ———, 124
Agnosticism, 140
Agudath Israel, 104, 159n
Aha, Rabbi, 159n
Ahurmazda, 34
Ain Yaakob, 155n
Akiba, Rabbi, 59, 60
Alexander, the Great, 4, 18, 63, 151n
    156n
    the spirit of, in the air of Palistine,
    24
Alexander Jannaeus, 26, 40, 41
Alexandria, 27
America, 138
Amon, 151n
Amos, 17, 20, 156n
Ancient Mariner, 137
Angel-Logos, 162n
Anointed, the Lord's, 19, 23, 35, 152n
Anthology of Wrath, 54
Anthropomorphism, 57, 163n
Antigonos of Socho, 43
Antiochus the Great, Epiphanes, 7, 15,
    16, 36, 38
Antiquities of the Jews, 148n, 151n,
    152n, 153n, 154n
Anti-Semitic,
    joke of Toynbee, 39
    rabidly, 80
Anti-Semitism, 26, 79, 151n
    crimes of Christian, 27, 79
    pre-Christian, 27
    Christian, 27, 30, 78, 80, 112
    Christian brand of, 77
    and demoralization, 81
Antithesis
    between Christian gentleness and
    Jewish violence, 51
Antonius Felix, 38, 153n
Apocalypse, 157n
Apostasy,
    Western Man's, 140
Aquinas, Thomas, 75
Arabs, 92, 93, 94, 95, 106, 131, 134
    Arab Legion, 93

displaced person, 95
heathen Arab tribes, 121
Aristobolus, 151n
Ashtoreth, 162n
Assimilation, 124
    of Jewry, 92
    in Eastern European countries, 93
Assyria, 63, 64
Assyrians, 17
Atomic Warfare,
    psychological consequences, 45
Attributes, Divine, 57
Augustine, 75, 90
Augustus, Divus, 23

Baal, 162
Baba Kama, Talmud Babli, 156n, 161n
Babylon, 104, 104
Baeck, Leo, 154n, 162n
Bar Kokaba, Kokba, 16, 37, 42, 95,
    104, 105
Berahot, Talmud Babli, 155n, 164n
Bereshit Rabba, 159n
Bergson, H., 85
Bevan, Edwyn, 155n, 156n, 158n
Bigotry, 26, 29
Black Death, 120
British, 93
Brotherhood of men, 24
Buber, Martin, 154n
Buddhism, 72, 163n
Burkhardt, J., XII, 161n

Caesaro-worship, 40, 153n
Caligula, 38, 39
Calvin, 90
Cambyses, 15
Catholicism, 90
Chaldeans, 17
Chance, omnipotence of, 16, 18, 21
Chmielnicki, 120
Chorinthians, Second Epistle, 46
Chosen People, 2, 12, 16, 23, 72, 76,
    157n
    and Jewish Universalism, 62ff, 64
    and religious dogma, 65
    covenant and responsibility, 67
Christendom, 80, 93, 144
    failure of Western, 50
    Western, 78, 94
Christian

166

167

and Torah, 69
Salvation of, 71
Jewry's negative attitude to, 75
Western Gentile world, 85
by culture, 85
Gentleness versus Violence, 71
"Ger Tsedek" the righteous Prose-
lyte), 68
Gerim, Talmud, 156n
Germans, 92, 93, 120, 132
Hitlerite German massacres, 93
and the guilt of the West, 109
Germany, 86, 165n
guilty, 109
Gessius Florus, 38, 153n
Ghetto, 87, 92, 105
Ghetto and Jews of Rome, 39   L
Gibbon, 165n
Glatzer, N. N., 164n
Gnostic sects, 161n
God,
the will of, XII
particular conception of, 2
Act of, 13
purification of parochial concept of,
17
the One True, of the Universe, 20
incarnate, 23, 76, 80, 99, 162n
as Power and not Love, 24
knowledge of, 46
Word of, 52
as Power and Love, 53ff, 56, 58, 77,
89
Israelitish, jealous, 53, 55
the Jewish, of the Old Testament,
and its readmission into Christianity, 30, 53
Mosaic and prophetic presentations
of, 55
diffraction of the unitary image of,
56
essence of, 57, 74
man's encounter wth, 58
Otherness of, 58
the Father, 58
Father, King, Creator, 59
's relationship to man, 59
's humility, 59
's infinitude, 60
Law of, 60
Universal Creator, 62
of the spirits of all flesh, 62
and universal creation, 63
's treatment of Israel, 65
the Living, 66, 150n
tribalized or egotized, 66
the fear of the Lord, 70
the voice of the Lord, 73

Law of, manifest in Creation, 89
the Will of ——— and the laws of
history, 101, 115
imitation of, 126
the nature of, 139
the Word of the Living, 147
the philosopher's, 156n
co-operation between ——— and
Man, 159n
's Transcendence, 163n
Goyim, 106
Grace, 89, 90, 110, 128, 130
Grand Inquisitors, 6
Great Britain, 134
Gregorovius, Ferdinand, 39, 123
Gregory VII, Pope, 88

Habbabuk, 156n
Hadfield, F. A., 158n
Hadrian, 15, 37, 42, 95, 107, 104, 119
Hadrianic persecutions, 59
Halaha, 117-18
Hallel, 158n
Haluts, 132
his Toynbean disillusionment, 132
Hasmonean,
prince, 5
princes, 28, 40, 41, 77, 116
dynasty, 40
princes, Hellenized Sadducees, 78
Hasting's Encyclopedia of Religion,
etc., 152n
Hay, Malcohn, 149
Hebrew, 86
tribes, early, 2
Hebrews, 155n
Hegel, 160n
Heilige, das, 155n
Heine, 85
Hellenic,
civilization, 4, 141
paganism, 23
motif in Christianity, 22ff
post-Alexandrine ——— society, 86
philosophy, 138-39
society, 143
Hellenism, 5, 6
the other tributary of Christianity,
25
Henry VIII, 41
Herford, R. Travers, 155n, 162n
Herakles, 23
Herod, 43
Herodianism, 45, 48, 69
Herodians, 117
Hillel, 20, 43, 44, 48, 118, 154n, 162n
Hinduism, 50, 72, 163n
Historian,

INDEX

Crux of a Christian, 72, 163n
the ———'s inspiration and the
Beautific Vision, 107
the terrible vision of the, 142
History, 153n
History,
central theme of, IX
laws of, X, 13
"is bunkum," X
a vision of God's creation on the
move, 13
law-making in, 49
not a Sunday School, 75
the abominable Age of Civilization,
etc., 98
as a study in Salvation, 98
the laws of History, 101, 115
success in, 122
continuity of Jewish, the, 134
ang guilt, 134
heroic perusal of the annals of, 144
debacle of Western, 165n
Hitler, 119
Hiya, Rabbi, 159n
Hobbes, 142
Holy Bible, Toynbee's on Judaism, 17
Holy Land, The, 104
Holy Spirit, The, 141-42
Homunculus, 98
Horney, Karen, 111, 113, 160n
Hosea, 17, 20
Humanitarianism, 98
Hume, David, 160n

Idumea, 77
Idumeans, forcible conversion of, 7
Ikhnaton, 151n
India, 138, 159n
Industrialism, 98
Inferno, The, 158n
Innocent II, Pope, 88
Inquisition, Spanish, 6, 7, 95, 107, 114
Portuguese, 95, 107, 114
Interpenetration, 128, 133, 146
Irenaeus, 56
Isaiah, 17, 20, 46, 63, 64, 82, 152n,
154n, 158n, 163n, 164n
Isis, Egyptian, 22
Islam, 5, 17, 50, 72, 93, 100, 127,
162n, 163n
politically debauched, 88
Israel, 63, 64, 73, 82, 124, 128, 134
a peculiar people, 64
and covenant, 67
and wife-beating, 86
impervious to alchemy of History,
101
redemption of, 130

Israelitish exiles, 143
Israel, the State of, 92
defended by force of arms, 93
successful response to disintegration,
108
Italy, 86, 87

Jacobs, Joseph, 158n
Jeans, Sir James, 158n
Jeremiah, 17, 20, 47, 64, 125, 126,
154n, 159n, 164n
and reckoning of spiritual values, 91
Jeremiah, Rabbi, 156n
Jerusalem, 11, 37, 38, 43, 45, 48, 69,
83, 102, 118, 147
challenge of the fall of, 118
Jesse, 47
Jesus, XI, 12, 13, 22, 48, 55, 58, 63,
73, 75, 82, 83, 84, 90, 98, 120,
125
birth story of, 23
Gentile descent of, 24
Galilean step-child, 24
a Galilean Aryan, 25
gentleness of, 42
response of, and his disciples, 46
against the Pharisees, 54
faith in, 70
original intention of, 76
crucifixion of, 80, 81, 165n
recoil of the shedding of his blood,
81
imitation of, 141-43
a Jew, 145
the source of the human inspiration
in, 151
Jewish,
Sicarii, 6
world-embracing ambition, 8
religious genius, 9
Messianism, 11, 20, 21
Satanic *emeutes,* 12
creativity, end of, 12
Messiah, 13
world dominion, 21
Futurism, 22
prophet, Galilean, 25
empire in the spiritual dimension, 25
vein in the Christian religion, 26,
27, 28
pople refuse dictation to conscience,
40
Robin Hood, or Davy Crockett, 42
response, 46
origin of Christian ethos, 48
three forms of Jewish reaction, 48
insurrections, 49
Bible, 54, 77, 89